What Would Bonhoeffer Say?

Al Staggs

WIPF & STOCK · Eugene, Oregon

Wipf and Stock Publishers
199 W 8th Ave, Suite 3
Eugene, OR 97401

What Would Bonhoeffer Say
By Staggs, Al
Copyright©2012 by Staggs, Al
ISBN 13: 978-1-5326-7130-2
Publication date 9/26/2018
Previously published by Intermundia Press, 2012

To

Harvey Cox

TABLE OF CONTENTS

N THE FIRST DAY OF May, 1988, I performed my original one-man play entitled *A View From the Underside: The Legacy of Dietrich Bonhoeffer* at the First Baptist Church of Portales, New Mexico. During the ensuing years I have presented the play at churches, colleges, and conferences throughout the United States and in Canada, Poland, Germany, and Switzerland. After most performances of the play I conduct question and answer sessions regarding the play's content, and there are two questions that are invariably asked.

The first question has to do with what Bonhoeffer would say about the role of the church in America and about some of the issues that have plagued America during the years following his death, such as the racism that is still rampant in this country, America's wars of choice, our nation's military and economic policies, and the disparity between the wealthy and the poor. I wrote this book as an accompaniment to my play in order to address that question.

I am a white male who grew up in segregated Arkansas and received a master's degree from Southwestern Baptist Theological Seminary. For twenty years I was a minister in various Southern Baptist churches. Therefore, the second question I am most frequently asked is how a person with my background became interested in the issues of peace and justice in general and in Dietrich Bonhoeffer in particular.

My introduction to Dietrich Bonhoeffer came rather late in my educational and theological journey. In the spring of 1983 I had the privilege of continuing my theological education at Harvard Divinity School under the auspices of the Charles E. Merrill Fellowship. As a Fellow of Harvard I had the opportunity to attend any classes of my choice within the Harvard system, with the exception of those offered by the medical school. In addition, Merrill Fellows were given the option of choosing their theological advisor from among the distinguished faculty of the School of Divinity.

During the year prior to my fellowship, I had read articles and books concerning the advent of a new theological system called "Latin American Liberation Theology." A course by this title was offered in the spring semester at Harvard Divinity School under the direction of the Divinity School's most noted professor, Harvey Cox. Professor Cox, whom I would choose to serve as my advisor, was skillful in helping his students understand the basis of Liberation thought. It was through a combination of reading the remarkable texts on the Theology of Liberation, Cox's scintillating lectures, and my own interaction with this world-renowned professor that I began to take a new look at my Southern Baptist legacy, my identity as a white male growing up in the South. I also began to reconsider my presuppositions about what the Bible was saying to me and to my world.

The Bible, which had become so familiar to me as a result of years of Sunday School, Vacation Bible School, and seminary training, suddenly began to take on a radical new meaning for me. The prophets from the Hebrew Bible had been there all along announcing God's impatience with systems and cultures of injustice. As I reviewed the Gospels, I was shocked at the radical teachings that had been completely ignored or glossed over in my own religious education. Why had I never before heard Matthew 25:31–46? I could not recall ever hearing a single sermon based upon this powerful and important text. Wasn't this a pivotal concept in the teachings of Jesus as to his level of identification with the poor and oppressed of the world?

I then took a new look at the Gospel of Luke and saw for the first time the preponderance of teachings regarding the rich and the poor. Where had all of this been hiding during all of my years as a Baptist and a student at a Baptist college and seminary? The Bible was suddenly a radical, even revolutionary text that seemed threatening to the status quo with which I was so well acquainted. Even in the familiar Magnificat in Luke there was a sense of the revolutionary in the advent of the Kingdom of God. Suddenly, with the help of Liberation Theologians, I was beginning to see the biblical account of the birth of Jesus and Mary's announcement in an entirely different manner.

Sometime during the spring of 1983, a light was turned on for me and a whole new understanding of my southern Bible Belt culture, with its religious conservatism, was revealed to me. I had always assumed that I was especially favored in God's sight as I was white, male, American, and a "saved" Baptist. What I had assumed was that I possessed the truth of God's Word in my life since I had always given assent to the absolute truthfulness and reliability of the scriptures. After my exposure to Liberation Theology and the teaching and guidance of Harvey Cox, it dawned on me that there was a new way of looking at both the world and the scriptures. What I began to feel during that spring was that there was a need within me to undergo still another kind of conversion. What I needed was to see who I was in relation to other groups and classes of people and to learn to listen to other kinds of people in order to help change the systems of injustice that have existed for generations.

Studying the life of Dietrich Bonhoeffer helped me to see and understand that a person who has historically represented a privileged and oppressive class could do something that is liberating for other people, for those who are oppressed. Here was a theological giant, notable among church leaders throughout the world and thoroughly ensconced in a culture of privilege and academia, who sacrificed those privileges in order to speak and act on behalf of those who were not as fortunate. Dietrich Bonhoeffer became an example to me of how one might be able to live out the challenges posed by the theologians and church leaders of Latin American Liberation Theology. I had been discovering new truths in my reading of the Liberationists but had been unable to discover how I might apply these new truths. Bonhoeffer became my guide.

Pastor Bonhoeffer did not have the opportunity to fully develop in his writings all of the concepts that were changing him during the last years of his life. He was too busy living out the demands of his new understanding in a context of extreme crisis and danger. His life and his sacrifice became his definitive volume of theology. His choices and his deeds confirmed his theological convictions and statements. Pastor Bonhoeffer was faithful unto death to the light that led him.

As a Southern Baptist pastor, I had observed the wrangling

and fighting of the Southern Baptist Convention for more than five years. Throughout those years the controversy had centered on the subject of theological correctness and orthodoxy. All of this tumult seemed to be theological hairsplitting, with no prophetic resolutions or courageous statements about some of the more challenging concerns of ordinary Americans, such as health insurance for underprivileged citizens and the economic plight of so many poor families in the United States. In direct contrast to Bonhoeffer's concerns and sacrifice, Southern Baptists leaders appeared to have no interest in relevant issues.

One of the sickening aspects of the fighting was that both moderates and fundamentalists expended so much energy and concern about the issue of power and who was going to control that gigantic denomination. This power struggle struck me as antithetical to the convictions and courageous actions of a man who was willing to relinquish every semblance of power in order to help those who were oppressed. Ultimate control of the Southern Baptist Convention was achieved by carefully planned political tactics and brutal criticism of all those who stood in the way, which signaled to me that Baptists had become a dysfunctional family, an abusive family that could not face the reality that a divorce was desperately needed.

Convention Business

Embroiled in controversy,
expending energies on the doctrinal enemy,
organizing armies,
articulating their statements of faith
they launched bravely on the battlefield of heresy.

With sword in hand and determined spirit,
reputations and characters were the resultant
casualties of this tumultuous affair.

Accusations, defenses, claims, counter claims, slurs,
hostilities, reprisals, recriminations,
all in the name of the Word.

The pagans said, "Good Show, Good Show.
Notice the Christians, how they slay one another."
The fight waxed heavy, while the Demon of Darkness
roamed the streets with freedom,
running over abandoned positions of defense,
the defenders having left to fight
the more important Doctrinal Battle.

There's a lull in the war with Darkness,
for the Christian soldiers are taking time out to
shoot one another.
Someone will win the battle,
but the war is in question.
Who will win the battle of Spirituality?
Who believes the Word more?
Ah, these are the important things.
Let the Demon of Darkness do his business
while we do ours.

The challenges I received from studying the works of Liberationists such as Gustavo Gutierrez, Jon Sobrino, and Ernesto Cardenal caused me to begin reading the Bible with new eyes and a new perspective. What a contrast their insights were from the empty talk about whether the Bible was "inerrant." These writers were helping me to see that history has always had a "view from the underside," the view of those who are traditionally the oppressed.

It was interesting for me to observe how the Fundamentalists of the Southern Baptist Convention continued to interpret the place of women, one of the historically oppressed classes. While the Liberationists were helping me to fully appreciate the revolutionary statement of the Magnificat by Mary and the noted place of the prophetess Anna in the Gospel of Luke, the Fundamentalists were vigorously defending their views on the submission of wives and their refusal to allow women to serve in places of leadership within the church. It was abundantly clear to me that the views these Fundamentalists were espousing were cultural views, not biblical views, for the Bible truly does not support such oppressive concepts.

This fundamentalist concept of women is similar to the traditional view of African-Americans and Jews. Until recent years fundamentalist Southern Baptists based their racist views on spurious interpretations of scripture. It is the same with Jews. For generations Baptists have caricatured Jews, basing these caricatures upon their interpretations of several New Testament texts.

In writing about the influence of Bonhoeffer, Eberhard Bethge describes his views of what religion had become,

> Religion has become essentially a way of distinguishing people. A victim of its divisive privileged character, it has presided over a vast number of acts of violence throughout history: Christians against non-Christians, theists against atheists, or whites against coloured people.*

From my study and reading of Latin American Liberationist texts I could better understand my own traditional Baptist and conservative perspectives and I could better understand what it was about my tradition that was deeply troubling me.

The rise of the Moral Majority during the late 1970s also played a major role in the development of my interest in Bonhoeffer. As I studied the phenomenon of the Religious Right, I became more and more convinced that this group resembled the German Christians during the reign of the Third Reich. Like the German Christians, the Religious Right is extremely patriotic. Like the German Christians, the Religious Right seems more concerned about private moral issues than issues that relate to the welfare and rights of the poorest people in the land. Like the German Christians, the Religious Right desires to keep its place of prominence and influence in national politics and with national political leaders.

It is rather strange that what I have discovered about myself in the last several years is that I am still a conservative Baptist from Arkansas who, at a very early age, felt a call to ministry and mission. That early conviction is still within me. What has changed is that there is now a different expression of that conviction. The focus and beliefs of this new conviction would be viewed in the eyes of many as being "liberal" in nature. There is a statement attributed to the late T. B. Maston, a longtime distinguished professor at Southwestern Baptist Theological Seminary, which is pertinent at this point. Maston said, "Be conservative in your interpretation of scripture and be liberal in your application."

In my characterization of Clarence Jordan, I interpret his written views as follows: "I'm convinced that Jesus was a raging liberal. Yes, he was a raging, sold-out, thoroughgoing liberal. 'Cause you don't get put on no cross for being a conservative!" These are my sentiments exactly. I am a liberal who is conservative in my view of scripture.

My Dad was an alcoholic, addict, and "rageaholic" who had little time for churches and even less for preachers. I always say that he was a reverse of Will Rogers in that he never met a preacher he liked. To Dad, preachers came across as being arrogant and close-minded. I think that he was at least partially correct. In truth, we ministers and church members should always be open to the possibility of seeing life and our scriptures in a whole new way.

Discovering Bonhoeffer shook me at my foundations and yet took me back to the simple conviction that there was truth in what I had committed my life to in the mid-1950s. What I needed to do with much of that "Christian culture" I had assimilated was to turn it on its holy head.

Although Bonhoeffer was executed in 1945, his theology continues to be relevant to the critical issues of religion, socio-economics, justice, and politics.

NOTES

* Eberhard Bethge, *Dietrich Bonhoeffer* (New York: Harper & Row, 1985), 780.

CHAPTER 1

HOW COULD THE HOLOCAUST
OCCUR IN A CHRISTIAN NATION?

First, I must try to explain the unexplainable, and that is this: how could a nation that could proudly boast of sons such as a Beethoven, a Goethe, a Schiller take part in atrocities against humankind? Tell me, how could a nation that could literally claim centuries of "Christian" history—how could that nation commit genocide?

OW COULD SOMETHING AS dreadful as the Holocaust occur in a nation like Germany, where there was no shortage of churches or Bibles, no shortage of professing Christians? One might have expected something as cruel as the Holocaust to come from a nation that had no history of Christian influence, but not from a nation such as Germany. After all, this was the land of Martin Luther. But as we shall discover later, not even Luther was exempt from murderous hatred of the Jews.

The question of how this could happen in Germany has been posed to me on numerous occasions during my years of performing and lecturing at churches, synagogues and colleges. Some insight on this question came as I reflected on my childhood in the state of Arkansas. I was born in 1946 and can remember how life was before the days of integration. My memory harbors vivid pictures of attending an all-white school system and attending an all-white church. When we traveled the ten-mile journey from our house to Little Rock, we would see the conspicuous sign at the front of the bus that informed "colored" people that they were required by law to sit at the back of the bus, behind the white line. The Trailways bus station in Little Rock had segregated restrooms for "colored" women and "colored" men. The water fountains were also segregated and clearly marked. As children we were told by our family, by our society, by our school, by our neighbors and friends, and by our church that "colored" people had "their place." I realized early on that a colored person's place was inferior to the place of the white person.

Where was the sense of the prophetic in the life of the white church that would question this culture of segregation? As a child, never once did I hear a minister challenge the assumptions of white people. On one occasion in 1957, a black woman attempted to enter our church on a Sunday morning. The pastor and deacons blocked her path and closed the doors on her. No black person was allowed to worship at my home church, the Highway Baptist Church of McAlmont, Arkansas. This was the church where I was taught the truths of scripture, the church where I had made my profession of faith just a year earlier.

In one particular discussion in Sunday School at Highway Baptist, the teacher, a deacon's wife, explained to her class of young adults the difference between a "nigger" and a "Negro." A "nigger" was someone who was "uppity," a troublemaker; and a "Negro" was a kindhearted, decent person who knew his or her place.

Baptists in Arkansas claimed they had a strong theological basis for their views on absolute segregation. During the early 1950s, Arkansas Baptists published doctrinal tracts that outlined the biblical basis for segregation. These tracts provided the reader with numerous "proof texts" for the practice of segregation.

There was one notable exception among white evangelical leaders during the struggle for integration in Arkansas. That person was Dr. Dale Cowling, the pastor of the Second Baptist Church of Little Rock. During the Little Rock Central High School crisis, Dr. Cowling stood in his pulpit one Sunday and declared that segregation was a sin. Second Baptist Church immediately lost a huge portion of her membership as a result of Dr. Cowling's statement.

Reflecting on those early years of blatant segregation, I remember that this is the same South where slavery had been so firmly entrenched for generations. This is also the South that has been traditionally identified as the "Bible Belt." There has never been a lack of churches or Bibles in the South. Yet it is in the South that slavery and segregation could thrive. Just as we pose the question regarding the Holocaust and Germany's Christian churches, we could also ask, "How could slavery and segregation exist in a culture that was so historically Christian?" As Walter Rauschenbusch observed, "After all of the revivals in the South, slavery was not extinguished."

My partial answer to this riddle is that this phenomenon points to what I term the "Principle of Immunity." If a young child is prescribed antibiotics for every little sniffle and cold, that child is likely to develop immunity to the healing effects of that antibiotic. The same could be said of any culture. If a particular society has been familiar with biblical teachings for generations, there is a danger that this culture can become immune to the true radical nature of Christian discipleship.

Clarence Jordan once reflected upon the time when he learned the song "Jesus Loves the Little Children." Thinking back to the words of that song and the culture that he knew, Jordan wrote in his personal journal:

The question arose in my mind, "Were the little black children precious in God's sight just like the little white children?" The song said they were. Then why were they always so ragged, so dirty and hungry? Did God have favorite children? I could not figure out the answers to these questions, but I knew something was wrong. A little light came when I began to realize that perhaps it wasn't God's doings, but man's. God didn't turn them away from our churches—we did. God didn't pay them low wages—we did. God didn't make them live in another section of town and in miserable huts—we did. God didn't make ragged, hungry little boys pick rotten oranges and fruit out of the garbage can and eat them—we did. Maybe they were just as precious in God's sight, but were they in ours? My environment told me that they were not very precious in anybody's sight. A nigger was a nigger and must be kept in his place—the place of servitude and inferiority.*

"Christian" cultures or societies can actually uphold the most horrific systemic injustices and claim that the way things are is the way they ought to be. The way things are, the status quo, can become "traditional moral values" because these traditions are time-honored and Christian-based, even Biblically-based in the eyes of many Christian people and ministers. This Principle of Immunity can also be illustrated through an example from my childhood. There was a train track located very near my home. I heard that Missouri Pacific train so many times each day and night during my childhood that I ceased paying attention to each passing of a train. On one occasion, a friend who lived several miles from my house was spending the day with me. At one point in our playing together, a train traveled by. My friend suddenly stopped and said, "Look, a train!" I had lived in this location for so long and had become so accustomed to the sounds of the train that I didn't really hear this particular train that passed by during our playtime. The same could be said of environments where Christianity becomes second nature, cultures where the Bible is read, preached and taught regularly. A culture can then cease "hearing" the message of the scriptures.

Much of the conflict that Jesus incurred in his ministry came as a result of the resistance offered by the religious establishment of his day. Traditionally, Christianity has leveled the charge of legalism against Judaism because of the responses Jesus received from so many of the religious leaders of his day. The harsh responses that Jesus received are meant to be instructive that any religious establishment of any age can be resistant to the requirements of true discipleship.

The church, along with its traditions and practices, can find itself on the side of evil. On many occasions the church has become an agent for repression of human rights and an agent for persecution and bloodshed. Instead of working for the liberation of those who were oppressed, the church has often become an ally during inquisitions, conquests, slavery, repression, sexism, racism, anti-Semitism and the gross inequality between the rich and the poor. The Bible has been used to enslave peoples, to make their lives more difficult and to keep oppressed persons in their places. Scriptures have been used throughout history to conquer the identified enemies and to take all of their resources and leave their lives destitute and hopeless. Christians often point to the Bible as God's Holy Word; however, it has been utilized throughout history in some of the most godless ways. The Bible and the message of salvation have at times been co-opted to endorse the vilest of attitudes and actions against innocent peoples. Nothing is as evil as an act of violence being perpetrated in the name of God. This is the most demonic of all evils. In recent history we have seen the record of slavery and that institution being blessed by a Southern Bible Belt Christianity. How could a Southern culture ever delude itself into thinking that its souls were revived when black sisters and brothers were living in chains? What is so astonishing is that, after all these years, the Southern Christianity has not demonstrated any real remorse over the sins of the past. What has been evident is the intransigence of white southern males to let go of their attitude of dominance in culture and in the life of the church. Have there been any major resolutions of repentance by the major southern evangelical denominations? The Southern Baptist Convention passed a resolution only after such a statement had been debated, repressed or ignored for years.

Much of the answer to the question posed in the title to CHAPTER 1 can be deciphered in the nomenclature "Christian Nation." As will be explained in CHAPTER 5, much of the basis for the anti-Semitism in Germany came from Christian theology and the teaching and preaching in many of the churches in Germany. It was the presence of this perverse Christianity that actually sanctioned such hateful and vile attitudes toward Jews.

Notes

* Dallas Lee, *The Cotton Patch Evidence* (Americus: Koinonia Partners, 1971), 7–8.

CHAPTER 2

WHERE THE CHURCH SHOULD BE

The Church in Germany has become so "spiritual" that it has allowed the earth to go to Hell! Oh, I can imagine now that some pious soul would come and stand right in front of me and ask, "Well, Pastor Bonhoeffer, do you not believe in a literal hell?" And I would say I most certainly do, but I believe we Christians have either created a living hell for many people right here on this earth, or we have allowed it to exist by our apathy! The Church must come out of her stagnation and move out into the open air of intellectual discussion with the world and risk saying controversial things if we are ever to get down to the really serious problems of life. The Church was never intended to be on the outside of the village in some safe secure little haven. The Church belongs in the middle of the village, right where the crises and the challenges and complexities and dangers of life occur. The Church is really only the Church as it exists for others.

CLARENCE JORDAN ONCE SAID that we've reversed the incarnation. We've taken a little flesh and blood of Jesus and deified it. We've taken the humanity out it. He said that we have thus done more harm to Jesus in this way than if we had crucified the Lord ourselves. Jordan said that we build monuments to the spirit of Jesus and take away his humanity. The incarnation was a sign of God's presence "with us." Yet the way in which the Church incarnates today seems to be antiseptic, aloof, removed from the mess and dirt of daily existence. The Church has become a beautiful place with clean buildings and gorgeous carpets and tall, stately steeples and not a place where we feel we are understood in our sinfulness, our hurts, our tragedies. So many of the pronouncements of Southern Baptist resolutions, for instance, never seem to address the tougher issues of life.

A discussion of the Protestant cross and the Catholic crucifix is pertinent to this issue. Protestants use crosses, void of the representation of Jesus, in architecture and liturgy. Catholics, however, depict Jesus hanging on the cross with their crucifix. The removal of the crucified Jesus from our crosses is representative of what we Protestants do theologically in our churches. We have taken the suffering, agonizing Jesus out of the picture and presented a triumphant Jesus who is victorious over death, victorious over every trial, temptation and problem. In the midst of the world's problems of death, disasters, diseases and tragedies we all need to know that God is with us. The Church in Germany in Bonhoeffer's time was afraid to put her wealth and position in the place of harm in order to speak for the persecuted. The Church removed herself to speak only of "heavenly" things, issues that pertain only to soul salvation and the "spiritual" life. In one of his letters from prison Bonhoeffer said, "The church is concerned only for its own security. It is a heavy incubus of traditional ideas with no effect on the masses."[1]

The last twenty-five to thirty years have seen a dramatic increase in the migration of churches moving their facilities from historic downtown areas or declining areas to locations where the homes of affluent young families are located. It is astounding to see just how many older churches are seeking "greener grass" by buying property and building in new areas that are more affluent and more populated. All of this transition takes a great deal of financing, which compels churches to reach that many more families in order to pay for the move. To drive around and see these relocated churches is an education in economics and lifestyle. These churches appeal to the young and upwardly mobile families because they are located nearby and offer a wide variety of programs, activities and staff for the entire family. Also, churches are forced to compete with other suburb churches by providing ample facilities such as recreational buildings. All of this requires a lot of money. Raising this kind of money and pursuing these kinds of outreach and growth goals leaves very little time for ministering to the poor and certainly less time for becoming an advocate for the poor. It is true that where a church locates its building usually dictates its theology and its understanding of missions and ministry.

When I first began to perform the Bonhoeffer play, I sent a copy of my video to a leading Southern Baptist pastor in one of the southeastern states. A few weeks later I received a brief response congratulating me on my work and my interpretation of Bonhoeffer. At the end of the letter the pastor referred to Bonhoeffer's statement, "I think the church should sell all of her property and give the proceeds to the poor,"[2] remarking that such an opinion would not sit well with his church since his congregation had just recently embarked on a twenty-two million dollar building program.

Where should the Church be? Oakhurst Baptist Church in Decatur, Georgia, is a congregation that at one time had plans of relocating to a newer and growing area of the city. After a great deal of prayer and thought, the congregation decided that its mission was to be in the place where it had always been. Oakhurst has instituted creative ministries to the neighborhood and to the world from its modest and aging facilities. The same could be said of Calvary Baptist Church in Washington, DC. That congregation has maintained its presence and its witness in a community that is surrounded by poverty.

At one point in my ministry I was a staff member of a large Baptist church in Texas. During those years of my affiliation with this congregation, the church conducted at least three major building finance programs. These campaigns raised somewhere between four and five million dollars for new facilities. In just the last several years I have heard news that the congregation is planning to consider relocation to an area on the outskirts of the city. I could not help but think of the many millions of dollars that had been raised during the life of that church to build its present excellent facilities. Now the congregation will be required to invest more millions to purchase new and expensive property and build new buildings at a much higher rate of cost per square foot. No doubt the buildings will require the finest of furnishings, architecture, and grounds because of the environment and context of large, expensive new homes surrounding the church property. It is true that one's context tends to dictate one's theology, and that applies to individual Christians as well as churches.

NOTES

1. Dietrich Bonhoeffer, *Letters and Papers from Prison* (New York: Macmillan, 1971), 381.

2. Ibid., 382.

CHAPTER 3

THE CHURCH AND ITS PROPERTY

The Church should sell all of its property and give the proceeds to the poor.

WHAT DO YOU THINK BONHOEFFER would say to American churches today if he were alive?" When I hear this question I usually think of the epigraph by Bonhoeffer on the opposite page. Bonhoeffer did not have the opportunity to explain in more detail what he meant by that statement. It is quite evident from some other statements of Bonhoeffer, however, that he felt that the Church in Germany was more interested in accrual than in sacrifice for the sake of the needy and oppressed. I firmly believe that if Bonhoeffer were residing in the United States today, he would be horrified and disgusted by so much of what is represented as church.

One of the greatest moral challenges of the 21st century will be the problem of the disparity between the rich and the poor, the haves and the have-nots. More than forty million Americans are without health insurance. One in four children in the United States is raised in poverty. The present minimum wage cannot possibly pay the bills of a family of four even with both parents working full time. The more conservative churches in the United States have not yet addressed this growing moral crisis. Conservatives and fundamentalists have largely ignored the Bible's strong and resounding teaching concerning love of wealth and have dealt exclusively with "family values" such as homosexuality, prayer in schools and abortion. In the last several national elections, religious conservatives and fundamentalists have heavily supported the Republican platform.

The pastors of leading conservative churches are wary of speaking prophetically about the evils of stockpiling wealth because that would mean the withdrawal of significant monetary support from their building programs and their salaries. How can a church that continues to need more and more of the membership's money have anything to say about sacrificial giving and sacrificial service? The gross income of the largest churches in our nation and the salary packages that their pastors command are not grounds for bragging. They are instead an indictment on the misguided paradigms of what church should actually be in the biblical sense.

When one listens to the sermons of television evangelists and popular television pastors, there is not much being said about the plight of the poor or the widening gap between the rich and the poor. There is an astounding silence among the most popular ministers and pastors regarding the problems of the underpaid, the underinsured, the underfed of our nation and world. What we often hear and see instead is a gospel of wealth. The gospel that is so often heard from the better known public preachers is one that promises great blessings if the listeners will only give to God, which translates into billions of dollars going into the holdings of churches. Church business is big business these days in the United States. How do churches that are continually building buildings, buying property and expanding staff and programs relate to a populace that is becoming increasingly destitute? How do churches speak with credibility to those who live from check to check, those who are struggling under heavy debts, those single mothers who are trying to raise two, three or four children on minimum wage salaries, those who have no health insurance and cannot afford a doctor's visit, those who require medication but cannot afford to pay the pharmacy because again there is no health insurance to cover the pharmaceuticals needed, those who desperately need dental work but cannot afford even one office visit? What do we say to those in dire economic straights that is something more than "Things are going to look up sooner or later?" As the apostle James said, "Suppose a brother or sister is without clothes and daily food. If one of you says to him, 'Go, I wish you well; keep warm and well fed,' but does nothing about his physical needs, what good is it?"

Manning Marable explains to us that the growing class stratification cuts across racial boundaries. He cites Alan Wolfe, Director of the Center for Religion and American Public Life, who stated in a recent New York Times article that "The 1990s will be remembered as a time of Reaganism without Reagan . . . the incomes of the most affluent Americans have risen twice as fast as those of middle-class Americans." Marable goes on to point out that "Back in 1980, the average top corporate executive's salary was forty-two times higher than the median income of a factory worker. By 1998, the top executives were taking home four hundred nineteen times more than factory workers."[1]

During the time when welfare reform was being discussed, enacted and carried out, there were noted church leaders who said that the government should get out of the business of welfare since that was the business of the Church. Churches have not been willing to pick up the slack where the cuts in welfare have taken effect, however. What has happened, therefore, is that many Christians have given their support and their votes, either by assent or by silence, to policies that have had profoundly adverse effects on many millions of poor people in this nation. Economic injustice in the United States is not something that has been a priority for the Moral Majority or The Christian Coalition. When these groups tout a return to Traditional Moral Values, those values do not include the right to a livable wage and a lifestyle with some dignity. The Reaganism of the '80s was supported by the vast majority of conservative evangelicals. The sellout of so many conservative Christian leaders to the Republican Party from the late '70s to the present renders their potential for prophetic pronouncements null and void. The average American worker has not found a friend in Jesus, in the Jesus that these ecclesiastical fat cats talk about. For Jesus to become Immanuel, God with us, would mean that he would have to have been born in the Highland Park section of Dallas and have to have served as a slick young thirty-something pastor in one of the leading Southern Baptist churches in that Dallas suburb. What kind of Jesus does the average working woman and man see espoused in the bright, shiny, well-dressed spokesman who stands amidst all of the glory and spectacle of our stately church edifices? What does the Jesus born in a stable in Nazareth to a poor woman have to do with the style of "churchianity" that is presently being projected in American culture?

The Manger

Sweet Little Jesus Child
born in that manger on a cold dark night,
in a stable, an outbuilding for animals—
the King of Kings.

the Prince of Peace surprised the world.
He didn't come into the world
in the Kingly court or the Big City.
He was not born into riches,
but poverty.

No one had any room for his Mama and Daddy,
no place for him to stay.
What if it were today?
Where would he be born?
Would it be New York or
London, or LA, maybe
Rome, or maybe Paris,
do you think?

Who would be his earthly parents?
Doctors, lawyers, statesmen?
Do you think?

No.
If he were born today,
like he was then,
he would have been born
to lowly campesinos in Nicaragua.
He would have been born in the ghettos
of Johannesburg, or Calcutta,
São Paulo, or Juarez, or Detroit.

His parents would be among those whose
meager benefits would have been cut
by compassionate politicians.
He would have been born to refugees in El Salvador
fleeing from the threat of the Death Squads
who would surely have sought him out.

He would have been born to Ethiopians
trudging their way along a desert floor,
searching for food and shelter from the cold.
And would we notice him today?

No, not at all.

So why do we pay homage to the manger scene?
Ah, we pay our respects in our own way.
We neutralize its thunderous meaning.
We place it in our lovely homes
and lovely churches,
in the center of our thriving towns.
We make friends with the baby Jesus
and we rob him of his hostility
to our secure ways.

Dietrich Bonhoeffer's statement concerning the Church selling all of its property and giving the proceeds to the poor seems to be saying that the Church must be willing to accept the lot of those who are the poorest in any society. In this way the Church is not removed from the plight of the disenfranchised and therefore can speak with credibility and integrity to the underprivileged. Henri Nouwen spoke and wrote much about the importance of compassion in ministry. He liked to say that to practice compassion was to "suffer with," which is essentially what the word means. In order to suffer with or practice compassion the Church must be in a position to empathize, and it is difficult if not impossible to relate to the poor while the Church remains affluent. How can a wealthy or affluent church ever be able to feel true compassion for the economically disadvantaged if the Church cannot face her own addiction to materialism, to the god of Mammon. Baptist pastor and theologian Walter Rauschenbusch was a prophet to our nation during the late 1800s and early 1900s. Rauschenbusch spoke out vigorously against the sins of greed in American society. He could very well be called a theological antecedent of Dietrich Bonhoeffer. Rauschenbusch observed the economic plight of so many Americans and understood that this inequality between the very rich and the very poor was the result of sin operating under the cover of free enterprise and capitalism. Rauschenbusch's words are particularly relevant to our present economic and moral challenges:

> The chief purpose of the Christian church in the past has been the salvation of individuals. But the most pressing task of the present is not individualistic. Our business is to make over an antiquated and immoral economic system; to get rid of laws, customs, maxims, and philosophies inherited from an evil and despotic past; to create just and humane relations between great groups and classes of society. . . . Here is the problem for all religious minds: we need a great faith to serve as a spiritual basis for the tremendous social task before us, and the working creed of our religion, in the form in which it has come down to us, has none. Its theology is silent or stammers where we most need a ringing and dogmatic message. It has no adequate answer to the fundamental moral questions of our day.[2]

Bonhoeffer's call to the Church to relieve the suffering of the poor exemplifies the very best witness of the Hebrew and Christian scriptures. An example of this call to relieve the suffering of the poor and oppressed can be seen in Isaiah 58:

> They ask me for just decisions and seem eager for God to come near them. "Why have we humbled ourselves, and you have not noticed?" Yet on the day of your fasting, you do as you please and exploit all your workers. Your fasting ends in quarreling and strife, and in striking each other with wicked fists. You cannot fast as you do today and expect your voice to be heard on high. Is this the kind of fast I have chosen, only a day for a man to humble himself? Is it only for bowing one's head like a reed and for lying on sackcloth and ashes? Is that what you call a fast, a day acceptable to the Lord? Is not this the kind of fasting I have chosen: to loose the chains of injustice and untie the cords of the yoke, to set the oppressed free and break every yoke? Is it not to share your food with the hungry and to provide the poor wanderer with shelter - when you see the naked, to clothe him,

and not to turn away from your own flesh and blood? Then your light will break forth like the dawn, and your healing will quickly appear; then your righteousness will go before you, and the glory of the Lord will be your rear guard. Then you will call, and the Lord will answer; you will cry for help, and he will say: Here am I.

When one reads passages such as the one above and similar kinds of passages from Jeremiah and Micah, it is very easy to draw parallels to our present day culture of religiosity that is juxtaposed with the economic plight of so many millions of Americans. When the Church should be speaking out on issues relating to economics, there is noticeable silence. Where there is dire poverty and increasing debt among so many Americans, there is notable opulence and increasing wealth in the churches. Bonhoeffer indicted the Church of his day by saying, "The Church is concerned only for its own security." This indictment could also be leveled at American churches.

Shout It Again, Lord

Godly sort of folks I see,
running out in front of the political march,
waving banners for moral values,
carrying their half-read Bibles.
Godly, conservative, white-faced folks,
throwbacks to slave owners using the Word
to justify their deeds,
to numb their hearts.

Remember this!
Remember this!
Remember this!
No one—
not the curser,
not the drug addict,
not the drunkard,

not the prostitute,
not the murderer,
not the prayerless pagan—
no one,
no one
is as immune to the substance of the Word
as those who embrace that Word
and then live
lives of compassionless compromise—
those who preach a relative gospel,
those who espouse power
and never question,
those for whom wealth is a right
and poverty inconceivable.

Their Savior, their Lord preached
to his own hometown that he came
to bring good news to the poor,
to liberate the oppressed,
and he was nearly murdered.

That Savior should come again and
shout the message today, this year,
this next political year.
Shout the good news
to give hope to the poor,
the elderly,
the children,
the disenfranchised,
the immigrant,
the farm worker,
the disabled.

Shout the liberating good news
that change, that conversion
must come not only to hearts.
Change must come to the practices of
white-faced heirs of slave owners

> who are trying to bring
> slaves back to the plantations,
> who are trying to widen the gap between
> those who get what they want
> and those who do without.
>
> Shout it again, Lord.
> Shout it again, Lord.
> Shout it for our time!

In 1980 I conducted a survey of three of the largest churches in the Southern Baptist Convention. All three of these churches are nationally known congregations. The pastor of each of these churches has served as president of the Southern Baptist Convention in recent years. I asked each of the church's business mangers to provide me with statistics relating to the amount of money that their respective congregations received during the previous year and how much of that total amount received was spent for world hunger relief. The combined revenue of the three churches totaled more than twelve million dollars, and together they spent just over one hundred dollars on world hunger relief. All of these churches are traditional, conservative evangelical congregations with a history of having the leading number of professions of faith reported each year. What, however, does this kind of record reveal about our lack of understanding of a whole gospel for the whole person?

For all the noise that Baptists make about being "people of the Book," we do not seem to be preaching very much about the sin of greed. Yet Jesus talked a great deal about the evils of materialism, and he also noted the gap between the rich and the poor. The gospel of Luke, for example, is replete with allusions to the rich and the poor. First, in Luke 1, Mary, the mother of Jesus, gives us the words of The Magnificat, which has been called "the most revolutionary statement ever made." Mary says,

"He has brought down rulers from their thrones but has lifted up the humble. He has filled the hungry with good things but has sent the rich away empty." Luke 4 recounts Jesus preaching in his hometown of Nazareth in which he states that he has come to preach good news to the poor. In Luke 12 there is the Parable of the Rich Fool who is judged because, as Jesus said, "This is how it will be with anyone who stores up things for himself but is not rich toward God." In that same chapter Jesus encourages his disciples to "Sell your possessions and give to the poor." There is, of course, as cited, the story of the Rich Man and Lazarus in chapter 16. In chapter 17 Jesus speaks of the rich young ruler who was told to "Sell everything you have and give to the poor, and you will have treasure in heaven." The rich man became sad, as the passage states, "because he was a man of great wealth." Jesus adds, "How hard it is for the rich to enter the kingdom of God! Indeed, it is easier for a camel to go through the eye of a needle than for a rich man to enter the kingdom of God." In chapter 19 Zacchaeus, the tax collector, is held up as a model for repentance because he stated, "Look, Lord! Here and now I give half of my possessions to the poor, and if I have cheated anybody of out anything, I will pay back four times the amount."

In his book *A Theology of Liberation*, Gustavo Gutierrez cites a document signed by a group of Peruvian bishops which had this statement as part of its confession, "We recognize that we Christians, for want of fidelity to the Gospel, have contributed to the present unjust situation through our words and attitudes, our silence and inaction."[3] Liberationists are fond of pointing out what they call "institutional violence." This is violence that is foisted on families and individuals within those families who are left hopeless economically because of such horrendous systemic evils. This institutional violence is often exhibited in alcoholism, drug abuse, spousal and child abuse. If ministers and church people are going to continue to speak about the demise of the family unit, they should preach and talk about all of the issues that contribute to the destruction of families. We should talk just as loudly about unjust and unequal pay scales as we talk about infidelity and promiscuity.

Archbishop Oscar Romero was assassinated in 1980 as a result of his efforts to stand with the oppressed of El Salvador. Shortly before his death he stated:

> The church in Latin America
> has much to say about humanity.
> It looks at the sad picture
> portrayed by the Puebla conference:
> faces of landless peasants
> mistreated and killed by the forces of power,
> faces of laborers arbitrarily dismissed
> and without a living wage for their families,
> faces of the elderly,
> faces of outcasts,
> faces of slum dwellers,
> faces of poor children who from infancy
> begin to feel the cruel sting of social injustice.
> For them, it seems there is no future—
> no school, no high school, no university.
> By what right have we catalogued persons
> as first-class persons or second-class persons?
> In the theology of human nature there is only one class—
> children of God.[4]

During the summer of 1982, I had the opportunity to visit with Southern Baptist missionaries from Central America at a missions conference at the Glorieta Baptist Conference Center in Glorieta, New Mexico. One morning I visited with one of the missionaries who was retiring after more than thirty years of service to one of the Central American nations. I asked him what he thought of the assassination of Archbishop Romero two years prior to this conference. He said, "Well, that's what happens to people who become involved in communism." I was appalled and stunned at this statement, for I had read numerous reports from other Christian groups that honored the work of this great priest and archbishop. I told the missionary that his view was not a view shared by other Christian groups. He was extremely agitated that anyone would think Romero was just working for the rights of the poor. In my disgust with this Baptist missionary I asked, "Well, I suppose that you had many friends among the aristocracy, didn't you?" He said to me, "That's how you have the opportunity to witness in these countries. You can't just go in there and act as if you know everything. It takes time before the leaders begin to experience conversion so that injustices can eventually and gradually be rectified."

This philosophy of mission work has unfortunately been the operative philosophy of Southern Baptists and other evangelical denominations for many years. This is the kind of evangelism that will choose to say nothing in the face of injustice so the Church will continue to have the freedom to preach and conduct religious work without interference from the state. This philosophy of missions and evangelism relies on maintaining the status quo. This kind of evangelism has nothing in common with the biblical concepts of costly discipleship or of true justice. The mission philosophy of saying nothing against injustice amounts to complicity with injustice. The Church's place is maintained off the backs of innocent oppressed people and the Church then becomes part of that oppressive system. The Jesus who is preached by this kind of dualism is not the Jesus of the Bible who identified with the poor and oppressed. This is not the Jesus of the Bible who gave hope to the downtrodden. No, this Jesus who has been preached by missionaries co-opted by the power of the state is the same Jesus who was preached for centuries in the white churches of the South. This is the Jesus who was preached in so many of the German churches during the years of the Third Reich. This Jesus is not Jesus at all.

Earlier I mentioned Archbishop Romero and the fact that even in his martyrdom he was accused of being a communist by one of our long-time missionaries to Central America. For the past few years I have been researching Romero's homilies in order to perform a one-person characterization of his life and ministry. To read his homilies is to be reminded of Dietrich Bonhoeffer. One sees in Romero's homilies just how rigorously biblical he was in his interpretation and application of scripture. His messages and his martyrdom are a resounding indictment of those missionaries who refuse to stand up for the rights of the poor and oppressed. The following is a portion of a message Romero preached on April 16, 1978:

> A church that doesn't provoke any crisis,
> a gospel that doesn't unsettle,
> a word of God that doesn't get under anyone's skin,
> a word of God that doesn't touch the real sin
> of the society in which it is being proclaimed—
> what gospel is that?
> Very nice pious considerations
> that don't bother anyone,
> that's the way many would like preaching to be.
> Those preachers who avoid every thorny matter
> so as not to be harassed,
> so as not to have conflicts and difficulties,
> do not light up the world they live in.[5]

In a message preached on September 9, 1979, Romero delivered a stinging indictment against much of what passes as religious education, as follows:

Unfortunately, brothers and sisters, we are the product of a spiritualized, individualistic education. We were taught: try to save
your soul and don't worry about the rest. We told the suffering:
be patient, heaven will follow, hang on. No, that's not right,
that's not salvation! That's not the salvation Christ brought. The
salvation Christ brings is a salvation from every bondage that
oppresses human beings.[6]

When the Church becomes addicted to money and materialism, it loses the ability to stand apart from the prevailing
culture of materialism and speak a prophetic word. The Church
subsequently becomes a part of the problem for the churchgoer
who is having difficulty making ends meet. Is giving to the
Church synonymous with giving money to God? That assumption could most certainly be challenged when one considers the
vast holdings of so many congregations in the United States.
Without a doubt, Dietrich Bonhoeffer would challenge the
American Church today to consider its worship of Mammon.

What Walter Rauschenbusch understood was that the
economic situation of a person or a family can lead to problems
with alcohol and drugs. When a person or family senses little
hope for escape from economic bondage and hardship, there is
a greater temptation to drown oneself in alcohol and drug use.
I still remember my father telling me that one of the reasons he
was so tempted to turn to alcohol was that he felt overwhelmed
at the thought of trying to earn enough money to support a wife
and five children. This kind of thinking is no excuse to turn to
the bottle; however, it is a very common temptation for those
who feel little hope economically.

The airwaves are glutted today with religious broadcasting,
yet there is virtually nothing being said on behalf of the plight
of millions of Americans who are struggling to pay bills and to
deal with a mountain of debts. For all of the religious talk that

we hear on television and radio, there is practically nothing being said by the religious organizations about the growing inequity between the rich and the poor.

When my first wife, Vicki, was diagnosed with metastatic melanoma in November of 1996, it was obvious to us that she would be required to quit working at her job with the San Antonio Independent School District. Vicki's salary was over $30,000 a year at the time she stopped working at the end of 1996. For the previous three years I had been trying, with some success, to build my career as a performing artist and had been performing sporadically. For the next year and a half I would become Vicki's primary caretaker. Her two insurance policies totaled more than five hundred dollars a month. Our daughter, Rebekah, would enter Baylor University as a freshman in the fall of 1997. How we managed financially during that time I do not know. During 1997 and 1998 the expenses took everything we had, our savings and ultimately all of my retirement funds. Of necessity my performing work slowed during those two years, as did my income. I was forced to not only dig into savings and retirement, but also felt it necessary to use my lines of credit in order to maintain our house payment, bills, insurances, and Rebekah's college education. In reality, our situation was not a unique one. There are millions of situations in our nation in which illness has forced families to rely on one income. A long-term or terminal illness can devastate a family's finances.

I recall meeting a seventy-five-year-old pastor a few years ago who told me that he would need to work until his death because he lost his savings and retirement funds as a result of his first wife's battle with Alzheimer's disease. He said that his wife had been ill for more than ten years, and her illness and the related expenses obliterated all of their financial holdings.

To meet the challenges brought by this alarming and escalating trend of disparity between those who have much and those who have too little, the Church must address the economic problems of people on at least three fronts. First, the Church must be honest about the evils of materialism in American society. The Church must be as forceful in preaching and teaching about greed as it is about sexual promiscuity. There is a notable silence in most churches on the evils of materialism and the love of money and possessions.

In recent years many Southern Baptist churches have participated in a program called "True Love Waits," a program to foster total sexual abstinence among teenagers. In one church I attended recently, all those youth who were vowing to remain sexually abstinent until marriage were asked to stand before the congregation and recite a vow of abstinence. They were given rings to wear that they would give to their future spouses as a sign of their sexual purity. I have no problem with the teaching of sexual abstinence; however, I do have a problem with singling out that temptation in this manner without also similarly addressing other sins such as the sin of greed. Richard Rohr has written an interesting piece called "The Three P's," which speaks forcefully to this subject:

> In the Sermon on the Mount, Jesus says there are three basic obstacles to the coming of the Kingdom. These are the three P's: power, prestige and possessions. Nine-tenths of his teaching can be aligned under one of those three categories. I'm all for sexual morality, but Jesus does not say that's the issue. In fact, he says that the prostitutes are getting into the Kingdom before some of us who have made bedfellows with power, prestige and possessions (see Matthew 21:31:32). Those three numb the heart and deaden the spirit, says Jesus. Read Luke's Gospel. Read the Sermon on the Mount. Read Matthew's Gospel and tell me if Jesus is not saying that power, prestige and possessions are the barriers to truth and are the barriers to the Kingdom. I'm not

pointing to bishops and popes. I'm pointing to us as the Church. The Church has been comfortable with power, prestige and possessions for centuries and has not called that heresy. You can't see your own sin."

The second way in which churches can address the problem of economic inequality is to structure more of their budgets to benevolence ministries. Presently, a majority of churches spend only a fraction of their annual receipts on anything having to do with benevolence such as a food pantry, clothes closet and utility and housing assistance. There are approximately 150,000 churches in the United States. If every church could sponsor one Habitat for Humanity house per year, there would be 150,000 fewer homeless families in the United States each year. That would mean that just over a half million people could be housed every year. Among Protestant churches there are more than 6,100 churches with over 1,000 members. Many of these churches could sponsor two or more houses per year with no difficulty.

Third, churches will be better able to address the economic suffering of Americans as congregations begin to reassess those expenditures that could be better spent on actual human need. If church staffs and congregations would begin to take a long hard look at the various ways in which their funds are spent, they could readily see the possibilities for diverting more money to such projects as Habitat for Humanity houses.

There is an anecdote from the life of Clarence Jordan which is particularly illustrative at this point. On one occasion Jordan was being given the grand tour of a magnificent and very expansive and expensive new church plant. The proud pastor of this church showed Jordan the large stained glass windows, the red carpet, the grand and costly organ with its massive pipes, the sanctuary that would seat several thousand people, the beautifully carved pulpit and the large choir loft that would seat hundreds of choir members. After touring the sanctuary and the modern and luxuriously furnished office complex, as well as a fully stocked gymnasium, the pastor took Jordan out on the front lawn and pointed up at the steeple of the church. He remarked proudly to Jordan, "Why Clarence, that cross alone cost us $75,000." Jordan considered the pastor's statement for some time, thinking to himself, "It seems like such a waste. How are they ever gonna get a man up on that cross since it's stuck way up there in the air so high." Finally, Jordan turned to the pastor and said, "I think you paid too much for that cross." The pastor asked, "You think so?" Jordan responded, "Yes, I think you paid too much for it. You know, there was a time when Christians could get those for free."[8]

In one of the many footnotes to Gustavo Gutierrez's book *A Theology of Liberation*, he cites a pastoral letter which came from one of the Latin American church groups. The statement reads, "One of the clearest signs of the evangelical independence and liberty that our church is meant to give would be the relinquishing of every economic tie with political power and the renouncing of every type of legal protection and privilege, including all the various rights acquired in the course of our history."[9] The document further states,

> The Church as institution must break off every concrete tie to any kind of public economic or social power, even at the risk of being persecuted and criticized or of losing economic resources or possibilities of support; it must do this in order to be always, like Christ, at the service of those who suffer, the poorest and most needy.[10]

NOTES

1. Manning Marable, "The Politics of Inequality," *The Black World Today*, January 2001.

2. Walter Rauschenbusch, *A Rauschenbusch Reader*. Ed. by Benson Y. Landis (New York: Harper and Brothers, 1957), 43.

3. Gustavo Gutierrez, *A Theology of Liberation* (Maryknoll: Orbis, 1973), 108.

4. Oscar Romero, *The Violence of Love*. Trans. and Ed. by James R. Brockman (Farmington: The Plough Publishing Company, 1988), 198–199.

5. Ibid., 44.

6. Ibid., 163.

7. Richard Rohr, *Radical Grace* (Cincinnati: St. Anthony Messenger Press, 1993), 18.

8. Dallas Lee, *The Cotton Patch Evidence* (Americus: Koininia Partners, 1971), 186.

9. Gutierrez, op. cit., 130.

10. Ibid., 130.

CHAPTER 4

HOW FAR SHOULD PATRIOTISM GO?

There is a strange phenomenon occurring in our nation. What is that phenomenon? Well, do you know that it is becoming increasingly difficult to be able to distinguish any difference whatsoever between the two allegiances that every Christian in Germany has—the allegiance to the Kingdom of God on the one hand and the allegiance to the state on the other? For some Christians these two are exactly one and the same thing. What I am trying to say is this: we in Germany are rendering to Caesar some things that belong only to God. Isn't the first great commandment, "Thou shalt have no other gods before me?" And yet these German Christians, as we are fond of calling them in a pejorative sense, have gone to the extreme in their attempt to bring these two allegiances to the same level. Many of our pastors, in the attempt to demonstrate their absolute allegiance to Hitler and the Fatherland, have draped their entire church sanctuaries with the national flag, the swastika! Why, some of them have even draped that flag across the altar of our Lord and Savior Jesus Christ. Listen to me! No national flag belongs in a sanctuary! Why, you ask? The answer is quite simple. You see, whenever you start doing that, you can be quite certain of one thing: the purposes of the Kingdom of God will be co-opted by the purposes of the state. Mark my word!

rowing up as a Southern Baptist in Arkansas, I was accustomed to seeing an American flag positioned in the front of the church worship center. The American and Christian flags were always displayed prominently on the platform for all to see. In our summer Vacation Bible Schools we children would recite the three pledges, the pledge to the Bible, the Christian flag, and the American flag. In our young minds those three allegiances were on the same level. No one ever instructed us that any one of these allegiances was greater than the other two. As I reflect on my Southern Baptist roots, I am amazed that, with our historical position on the separation of Church and State, flags and pledges to the flag could so easily have found a place in our churches. I am convinced that a majority of Baptists, a majority of evangelical Christians would have difficulty distinguishing any difference in the level of their allegiance to the state and the Kingdom of God.

Many Christians would insist that one is faith-bound to follow the injunction of Paul as found in the thirteenth chapter of Romans. The first verse of that chapter states, "Everyone must submit himself to the governing authorities, for there is no authority except that which God has established. The authorities that exist have been established by God." Bonhoeffer understood this dilemma and referred to the First Commandment, "Thou shalt have no other gods before me." Bonhoeffer knew that it is idolatry for a nation to be given a position equal to the place of God in the allegiances of the people.

When I was pastoring in the mid 1980s, the Home Mission Board of the Southern Baptist Convention launched a nation-wide evangelistic program entitled, *GOOD NEWS AMERICA*. The Home Mission Board commissioned a special edition of the New Testament, which carried a striking cover. On the cover was a heart with red and white stripes to depict the colors and the image of the American flag. In the left corner of the heart, at the place where the fifty stars would normally be located on the United States flag, a cross had been substituted. Under this graphic logo were the words, "Good News America, God Loves You." The symbol was to me a clear misappropriation of both the cross and the flag of the United States.

I was one of a handful of pastors within the Southern Baptist Convention who protested the use of this logo. While I had no argument with the campaign itself, I vehemently opposed the message that the cover of this New Testament conveyed. In the fall of 1985, I brought this issue before my church to ask the congregation to vote on the matter as to whether we should utilize these specially bound issues of the New Testament from the Home Mission Board. The business session resulted in the church voting to use these spurious New Testaments. I was resoundingly outvoted. What made this all so particularly uncomfortable were the kinds of statements that I heard from people who spoke out vigorously for using these New Testaments. A number of the statements seemed to equate one's allegiance to one's country on exactly the same level as one's allegiance to God.

I recall a statement made by a Baptist friend, C. Welton Gaddy, on this issue. Gaddy explained to me that this issue was not going to be won by intellectual arguments, no matter how persuasive, as this was in the final analysis an emotional issue. He said that most Baptists would not be able to understand the reasoning of intellect because of the emotionally charged feelings surrounding the American flag.

Richard Pierard relates how the dean of the Magdeburg Cathedral reveled in displaying the Nazi flags prominently in his church. The dean stated, "Whoever reviles this symbol of ours is reviling our Germany."[1] Such a show of patriotism was not uncommon among churches in Germany during the years of the Third Reich.

Recently I heard a young Baptist college professor speak of one of his interim pastorates during the Desert Storm campaign. On the Sunday before the Desert Storm assault, he went to church early and discovered that the woman in charge of decorating the worship center had displayed the banner of each of the military services in the choir loft. She had also put the American flag on the Lord's Supper or Communion table. This is the same kind of excess that occurred in Nazi Germany when the swastikas were draped throughout many of the church sanctuaries.

Some years ago Eberhard and Renate Bethge made a visit to the United States. Eberhard was Dietrich Bonhoeffer's biographer and was one of his closest friends. Renate, Eberhard's wife, was Bonhoeffer's niece. The Bethges came to Lynchburg, Virginia, to visit with a renowned Bonhoeffer scholar who lives there. During their visit, the Bethges expressed a desire to visit the worship services of the Thomas Road Baptist Church in Lynchburg where Jerry Falwell was pastor. The American scholar informed the Bethges that he was not a fan of Falwell and did not plan to attend one of Falwell's services but that he would be most happy to drive them to and from the church on Sunday morning. The scholar dutifully delivered the Bethges to Thomas Road Baptist Church and then picked them up following the worship time. When the Bethges came out of the service, Eberhard was sporting a pin of an American flag on one lapel and a pin of a cross on the other lapel. Bethge remarked to his American scholar friend, "They just don't get it, they just don't get it."

Pious Patriotism

Ole preacher Robertson,
Why don't you take your religious brand
to El Salvador?
Walk through the shattered villages,
the bloody alleys.
Tour the simple graveyards
of victims, thousands of victims,
who have been affected by our military might.

Ole preacher Robertson,
I'm sorry there are no cameras
in El Salvador,
so I guess you won't be going.
Simple answers with grave consequences.
Pious platitudes with no biblical basis.

Keep smiling, preacher Robertson.
Keep your deacons happy, too.
We know you pay a price for your
brand of discipleship.
All I ask is that you please

get the flag off of the Bible!

Smiles, fatter faces, bigger churches;
smiles, bulging profits, bulging prophets
with three-piece suits,
toothy smiles with instant answers,
soothing souls and pounding
on their pulpits.
Wavy hair, brushed straight up,
prophets loved by nearly everyone who is anyone.
No cross for these boys;
they own the crowd.

Smiling faces, bigger budgets.
Another groundbreaking, money's flowing in.
Pompous souls who speak so sure.
Go on, prophet,
Tell them what they want to hear.
Select the sins you disdain so carefully.
The people love your golden chandeliers.
They love the stately steeple,
and the parlor is a lovely place.

Down in El Salvador all hell has broken loose.
Prophets there are killed.
They couldn't make it with the right folks.
Too much gospel for those leaders to endure.
Hard to find smugness there,
not too many fattened faces,
three-piece suits are in short supply.

You've got to make alliances
if you're going to be a
great American prophet.
How do you think you get big churches
with beautiful buildings and beautiful people?
Alliances have to be made.
That's the problem with those

slaughtered prophets down in El Salvador.
They don't know how to make alliances,
they've only made them with the poor.
Tickle our ears, brother preacher,
with devotions of goodness and love.
And talk of the sins of others, those
whoremongers, drunks, gays and pagans.
The preacher, a man who's paid
for being good,
which means he doesn't threaten.
A man who needs to be needed
and loves to be loved and adores being adored.

Some sin is obvious for all to see
and so easy to address.
Other sin is hidden, subtle, but just as deadly.
The sins of pagans do not surprise.
It's the sin of good folk that confounds me.

They read a Bible without error
but omit the word "compassion."
They talk about the world's misery
But don't, God forbid,
Suffer with the miserable.
With their condescending air
they pass out aspirin to the starving
and pious phrases to the oppressed.
The comfortable ones say,
"Changed lives are what they need to
deliver them from their poverty."
But change is what the good folks need.
Yes, "even saintly folk will act like sinners
when they haven't had their
customary dinners" (Brecht).

They long for deeper Bible studies,
so deep as to be detached.

Matthew 25:31-46 has been spiritualized,
neutralized and rendered null and void.
The least went begging—
"He did not regard equality
with God as a thing to be grasped."
Grasping has become a virtue.
Privileges are now retained for the fortunate few.
The offensiveness of the cross
has been softened,
co-opted by the sweet smell of success:
no one is offended any more.
The first shall be first and the last shall be last.
Violence is most subtle at the voting booths.
Christians have opted for their pocketbooks,
getting politicians to cut their taxes
and to cut welfare.
Good rich people getting handouts in tax cuts
while taking food from the defenseless poor.
It shall not go unnoticed,
but right now Lazarus is still
eating scraps from the table.
Justice is deleted from their Bibles.
Regard for the poor is a "liberal" notion.
Martyrdom is common to the
south of Fat Cat Kingdom.
The hungry campesinos gather to pray
in their stucco huts, while many miles away
fattened, carefree faces fill their marble halls
and give thanks for their fatness.

The death toll rises in the hinterlands
while the Grand Ole Church underwrites
a new expensive monument.
Show me the signs of the Christian occupation;
show me the signs.
Giant, empty shells of marble and concrete—
Monuments, idols, ornate meeting places,

museums, beautiful people
meeting in beautiful palaces
in worship of the carpenter's son.
The child of Mary, son of Joseph of Nazareth,
the one born in a stable.
Modes outshining meaning, religious rote,
sacred security in their "sanctuaries."
Basking in the music of grand choirs,
bombastic organs and golden bells,
singing songs with countless "alleluias"
while the prophets salved the
suffering consciences with a few selected verses.
"Los Pobres" have no hearing
in these holy, stately halls.

Raise our flag, raise our flag!
We chant in the face of all our injustice,
and we think that we are
God's most favored nation.

The time to observe the level of patriotism demonstrated in American churches is the Sunday closest to July 4th. It is not uncommon to see gigantic flags displayed prominently in the church worship centers, accompanied by patriotic hymns and even by the singing of the national anthem. In a former church I attended, the minister of music installed an extremely large American flag over the baptistery, in which a depiction of Jesus as the Good Shepherd was painted. The covering up of the Good Shepherd mural by the flag was particularly symbolic.

NOTES

1. Richard V. Pierard, "Radical Resistance," *Christian History* (Vol. X, No.4, 1991), 30.

CHAPTER 5

CONFESSION OF GUILT

The Church confesses her timidity, her evasiveness, her dangerous concessions. The church has been untrue to her office of guardianship and to her office of comfort, and thus she has denied to the outcasts and to the despised the compassion that she owes them. To put it another way, the Church has failed to speak the right word, in the right way, at the right time. She has just stood by while violence was being committed under the very name of Jesus Christ. Therefore, she is guilty of the deaths of the weakest and most defenseless brothers and sisters of our Lord Jesus Christ.

N O OTHER STATEMENT BY Bonhoeffer sums up so succinctly and so dramatically the nature of the complicity of guilt that would be laid at the feet of the Church in Germany in the deaths of six million Jews during the Holocaust. Bonhoeffer clearly points the finger of accusation at the Church's silence, apathy and even active complicity as the primary cause for the deaths of the "brothers (and sisters) of our Lord." Bonhoeffer is, of course, referring to the fact that Jesus was a Jew.

Bonhoeffer once remarked that when the state crushes innocent victims beneath its wheel, it is up to the Church to put a spoke in that wheel. There were exceptions, rare exceptions, of church leaders who spoke out for the Jews; however, the vast majority was characterized by silence and active complicity with the Hitler regime.

This complicity of guilt of the Church crossed national boundaries. In 1934 the Baptist World Alliance found itself in a stormy controversy over whether this organization should hold its annual meeting in Berlin. After much debate, it was finally decided that Berlin would be the host city. One Southern Baptist leader, a state Baptist newspaper editor, wrote in his editorial following the meeting that Hitler was cleaning up the streets of crime and ridding the nation of pornography. He remarked that Hitler did not smoke or drink and that he was also a churchman. The editor's views toward the treatment of Jews carried no hint of sympathy for their plight.

What happened in Germany occurred as a result of the combination of forces of right-wing politics and right-wing religion. So many religious leaders in Germany felt that it was their moral duty to unflinchingly support the purposes of the state. A famous statement by the Church during that era was, "We will continue to preach the gospel of Jesus Christ and support the policies of the National Socialists (Nazis)."

In the late 1970s and early 1980s I observed a striking parallel to Nazi Germany in the United States. During the late 1970s, the Moral Majority became a powerful political force in this nation. It is fair to say that the election of Ronald Reagan over Jimmy Carter in 1980 was due in large part to the influence of the Moral Majority on so many voters. The Moral Majority, under the leadership of such church luminaries as Jerry Falwell, Charles Stanley, and D. James Kennedy, identified certain "traditional moral values" that they deemed could be better addressed by the election of a Republican president and other Republican candidates.

The moral issues that the Moral Majority considered of greatest importance were issues such as prayer in schools and abortion. What their moral agenda did not include was any mention of the plight of the poor in the United States or the fate of the refugees of El Salvador who were fleeing to the United States to escape violent forces, forces that were to a great extent trained and armed by our nation. In respect to the concerns of the Central American nations of Guatemala, Honduras, El Salvador and Nicaragua, the Moral Majority positioned its support behind the official and historical United States policy of promoting imperialism and subduing the voices of change. The Moral Majority endorsed our nation's support of the Contras in Nicaragua even though the human rights record of the Contras was horrific. In El Salvador, right-wing death squads carried out thousands of civilian murders. These death squads had been supplied and trained by the United States military, yet there was not a hint of outcry or criticism from the Moral Majority.

Iran-Contra conspirator Oliver North has been touted as a hero by the Religious Right for his part in helping to smuggle arms to the Contras in Nicaragua. John Hagee, the pastor of the large and well-known Cornerstone Church in San Antonio, invited North to speak from his pulpit several years ago and labeled him as "America's greatest Christian." In reality, North lied to Congress and helped to facilitate the deaths of many innocent Nicaraguan civilians because of the aid that was given to the Contras. President Reagan called these warriors "freedom fighters." Reagan was correct in his nomenclature but mistaken in his understanding of that term. The Contras were fighting against freedom, not fighting for freedom.

The election of 2000 proved to be another opportunity for the Religious Right to push for their "moral" agenda by the mass distribution of "voter guides" that were sent to a vast number of evangelical churches throughout the nation. Judging from these guides over the last twenty years, it would certainly appear that God favors the Republican Party and its candidates. Jerry Falwell made it very clear in the spring of 2000 that George W. Bush was "God's Man." Falwell also let it be known that he would work vigorously to help Bush get elected President.

James Dobson has served as one of the nation's leading spokespersons for the interests of the Religious Right. Just prior to the election of 2000, Dobson released a pamphlet in which he outlined the nine key issues that will shape America's future. These issues include: (1) the Sanctity of Human Life, (2) Abortion, (3) Physician-Assisted Suicide, (4) Homosexuality, (5) Sex Education, (6) Pornography, (7) Taxing Families, (8) Education and (9) Religious Freedom. As Dobson explains in his booklet, "Each (of these issues) is vital to our collective moral health. I have grouped issues in related categories and attempted to provide an overarching biblical perspective, grounded in a Christian worldview, for each category." The obvious question that comes to mind in reading this pamphlet is, "Where is economic justice to be found in the list of moral issues?"

On Sunday, November 5, 2000, two days prior to Election Day, I drove to some Southern Baptist churches in the Dallas-Fort Worth Metroplex to inquire about possible voter guides for the parishioners of the church. At one of the largest and most prosperous churches in the area I received a pamphlet published by the Texas Christian Coalition called a "Pro-Family Voter's Guide." The guide focused on the following issues:

Educational Choice for Parents (vouchers)
Unrestricted Abortion on Demand
Elimination of the Marriage Penalty Tax
Elimination of the Death Tax
Banning Partial-birth Abortions
Adoption of Children by Homosexuals
Prescription Drug Benefits for Medicare Recipients

The supposed views of each of the Presidential candidates, Al Gore and George W. Bush, were listed by each of the issues.

After consideration of this guide, one has to ask if there

were no other "moral" issues involved in this election. Certainly one issue that was not mentioned is the environment. Another issue that might have been raised is each candidate's views on a potential tax-cut and how that might affect those with low incomes. The voter guide did not address the issue of campaign finance reform, certainly a national moral issue, nor did it mention the death penalty. There was no mention of what each candidate might do to provide medical coverage for the more than forty million Americans who are uninsured. These are moral issues that should have found their places on that voter guide published by the Texas Christian Coalition.

One of the links mentioned on the web site of the Texas Christian Coalition is Billy Graham Ministries. One wonders whether Billy Graham actually agrees with the truncated moral vision of this organization, an organization that has clearly and unmistakably thrown its weight behind the Republican Party. On second thought, Billy Graham has never been one to speak out about the necessity for economic and social justice in any courageous, prophetic way. Those issues have somehow never found their way into Graham's sermons.

The Religious Right is consistent in the absolute refusal to say anything whatsoever about concerns that relate to economic and social justice. I have a theory about this amazing silence of the Religious Right on the subject of justice. My sense is that to speak truly prophetically about the great gap between the rich and the poor that exists in this nation would cost many of the empires of the Religious Right leaders their sources of income for their sizable operating budgets. To speak of the need for a decent living wage or to lobby for healthcare for more United States citizens would mean biting the hand that feeds them. It takes a lot of money to operate major evangelical churches and enterprises, and no one wants to offend major benefactors such as big business corporations. Could this be the reason why the candidates who are supported are Republicans? There is little doubt that there has been a marriage between conservative churches and the Republican Party.

CHAPTER 6

LETTER TO EBERHARD

My dear friend Eberhard, you recall that I wrote to you before concerning the Jewish question. It is my firm belief that the expulsion of the Jews from the West means the expulsion of Christ, for Christ was a Jew. November the ninth, 1938, the night of Crystals, the Night of Terror—Kristallnacht—when we good Germans destroyed so many Jewish houses of worship. And the thought of that occurring in a nation which has traditionally sung that little Christmas hymn, "Stille Nacht, Heilige Nacht." I shall never, ever sing that Christmas hymn again without first thinking of Kristallnacht.

HAVE NO IDEA WHAT ACTUALLY prompted me to merge the concept of the Christmas hymn "Silent Night, Holy Night" with Kristallnacht or the Night of Crystals. It did seem that the idea of the persecution of Jews by a predominately Christian nation was so irrational, so unthinkable, that nothing in that nation's Christian tradition could be considered sacred following the unspeakable horror of the Holocaust. Robert McAfee Brown writes that "The killers affirmed God in church, in their children's bedrooms, in the carols they sang at Christmas, and the hymns they sang at Easter—and they denied God by humiliating, torturing, and destroying a special group of God's children."[1]

In another part of the play *A View from the Underside*, Bonhoeffer relates to his audience a troubling dream that frequently visits him in his cell, as follows:

> In this nightmare I am awakened very early in the morning by what appear to be animated murals on the cell walls. On one wall there is a large choir of two hundred or more voices singing

the great anthems of the Church and in front of the choir is a minister in his long, flowing robe. As a kind of horrific paradox, I see on the opposite wall a ghastly picture of the death camps we good Germans have created! And there just staring at me are the hollow eyes of the victims! What I hear is a terrible cacophony of sound, from one wall the great anthems of the Church and from the other wall the cries of the victims.

Ah! Listen to me! Only those who cry out for the Jews may sing the Gregorian chants! Only those who cry out for the victims may sing those hymns of faith!

Christians have only just begun to face the manner in which the Bible has been used for centuries to stereotype Jews. Christopher M. Leighton states,

By insisting that biblical truth is fixed for all time, that the content of faith consists of immutable propositions, that the primary pedagogical task of the church is simply to pass on what it has received, conservative Christians have trouble acknowledging the severity of the problem. The tradition that caricatures Pharisaic Judaism as legalistic and spiritually vacuous, the tradition that holds the Jews responsible for "deicide," the tradition that claims that the "old covenant" is now obsolete and thus "targets" Jews for conversion—this tradition is anchored in the church's reading of the New Testament, and is therefore extremely difficult to criticize. When conservative Christians deliver this tradition to their children, they seldom recognize the cancer they have transmitted with the body of biblical truth.[2]

An example of the manner in which our traditional reading of the New Testament has been used to caricature Jews can be found in the Gospel of Matthew, Chapter 27, verses 24 and 25, where the Jews are quoted as saying, "May his blood be upon us and upon our children." Norman Beck tells us that "Matthew 27:24–25 is not a documentary of events but a literary composition that had as its purpose the removal of blame for Jesus's death from Pilate and Roman power and the transferal of guilt to all of the Jewish people forever." Beck reminds us that for nearly nineteen centuries Christians have considered these verses to be a record of what actually happened and therefore grounds for anti-Jewish attitudes and actions. The Holocaust has put this interpretation into serious question, however. Beck feels that this scripture is so problematic that we must consider relegating the passage, as with other anti-Jewish passages, to small-print status in our translations and usage.

Another example of traditional anti-Jewish interpretation of the New Testament can be found in 1 Thessalonians 2:13–16, where Paul says, "You suffered from your own countrymen the same things those churches suffered from the Jews, who killed the Lord Jesus and the prophets and also drove us out." Norman Beck offers several possibilities as to how the Christian community could deal with such anti-Jewish passages. First, he says that we could dilute the material that seems offensive and change "the Jews" of verse 14 to read "their political leaders." Secondly, we could retain the literal translation but place parentheses or brackets around verses 13–16 with footnotes explaining that these verses were probably added to the letter following Paul's death. A third possibility would be to relegate the verses to small print status. A fourth possibility would be to eliminate the verses from the translation altogether.[3]

Kristallnacht was, of course, the "Crystal Night" when the Jewish population was first terrorized on a massive and nationwide scale. That night numerous synagogues were burned. Bonhoeffer's response to this event is noteworthy. In the Bible that Pastor Bonhoeffer used for study, he underlined in Psalm 74, "They burned all the meeting places of God in the land," and wrote next to the scripture, "9.11.38." He underlined the next passage and put an exclamation mark: "We do not see our sign;

there is no longer any prophet, and there is none among us who knows how long." In a leaflet he sent to his Finkelwaldian students a few days later he wrote, "I have lately been thinking a great deal about Psalm 74, Zechariah 2:8 and Romans 9:4f. and 11:11–15. That leads us into very earnest prayer." He asked his students to look up the passages and take heed of the words, "He who touches you touches the apple of his eye." The crowning statement of the Romans passage can be seen in the eleventh chapter, verses 28 and 29: "As far as the gospel is concerned, they are enemies on your account; but as far as election is concerned, they are loved on account of the patriarchs, for God's gifts and his call are irrevocable."[4]

I recently heard a Southern Baptist minister speak of the Jews as being "lost," adding that they would not receive eternal life. Paul's teaching in Romans is a challenge to that widely held belief. What is so despicable is that Christian ministers have failed to be sensitive to our anti-Jewish and anti-Semitic interpretations of so many New Testament scriptures. Dietrich Bonhoeffer rightly referred to the Old Testament or Hebrew scriptures in his study Bible and in his circular to his students to teach another way of looking at Jews.

There is a crying need for a complete regeneration of Christian education, from the seminaries of our Christian denominations all the way down to the youngest children's Sunday School classes, regarding a more respectful view of the Jewish people. For the most part, churches and denominations are carrying on Christian education and seminary education as though nothing happened from 1933 to 1945. The Holocaust demands that Christians rethink our theology, doctrines, education, evangelism and preaching. Johann Baptist Metz rightly espouses the view, "Can our theology ever be the same again after Auschwitz?"[5] The truth is that our theological education has not recognized the hatred that has been fueled, to a great extent, by the Church. In respect to the Holocaust, Robert McAfee Brown determined that

> One who has seen even the periphery of the kingdom of night will never again feel fully at ease in the center of the kingdom of light. Which means that how we think, feel, react, struggle, love, engage, will all be subject to new beginnings. Old categories will be inadequate, new categories frightening."[6]

Brown quotes Wiesel, who says, "In the beginning there was the Holocaust, we must therefore start all over again."[7]

Starting over will necessitate identifying and isolating all of those New Testament passages, and there are many of them, which caricature Jews in a negative light. After the Holocaust, Christian pastors, teachers and seminary professors cannot read such scripture in their classrooms or pulpits without disavowing any Jewish stereotype or generalization of the Jewish people. To refuse to change our method of teaching and preaching in churches and seminaries signals that we Christians do not understand the connection between Christian anti-Semitism and the Holocaust. To refuse to change our interpretation of scriptures that put Jews in a bad light is also a signal that we are carrying on the same misguided tradition that existed in so many churches in Germany prior to and during the years of the Third Reich.

If we as Christians maintain that the Bible is Truth, we must do our homework and reform our preaching and our teaching to reflect that we take seriously the horror of the Holocaust. If we refuse to change our education and preaching in order to clear up long-standing misrepresentations of the Jewish people, we are no longer preaching and teaching anything that is close to resembling the Truth. Norman Beck rightly asks,

"What are we who live as Christians during the last decade of the twentieth century going to do about the anti-Jewish polemic in the New Testament, which has provided the theological basis for oppressive, unjust, and extremely hurtful anti-Semitism?"[8]

Dietrich Bonhoeffer's life and, more importantly, his death are symbols of the crisis of our theological status quo that has endured for centuries. There was nothing within the existing and accepted theological framework that could refute or effectively criticize the prevailing anti-Semitic views. There was nothing in Christian theology that could rightly identify Jews as the oppressed persons under the Nazi regime and under a "Christian" culture. These were the ones with whom Jesus would naturally identify, since they were both Jewish, like him, and victims, like him. This is a complete reversal of what most Christians have believed, that it is the Christian who has been the oppressed and that Jesus favors Christians above any other group of people.

As a beginning, Baptists and other Christian denominations should set aside a Sunday for remembering the victims of the Holocaust. This event should be as much a part of our liturgical calendar as Advent or Lent or Passion/Palm Sunday and Easter. To commemorate such an event would indicate that we Christians are finally beginning to take seriously our complicity in the suffering of Jews throughout history.

Dietrich Bonhoeffer failed to convince his fellow Christians of the danger of a Nazi regime. He was unable to speak as clearly as we would have liked for him to speak about the ghastly views of so many Christians within Germany. Bonhoeffer also failed in the conspiracy to bring an end to Hitler's rule. Bonhoeffer's failure was the failure of perhaps Germany's finest young theologian and churchman, as well as one of the brightest young stars in the entire world. His failures and his death were a sign that a new Reformation had come of age. Bonhoeffer's struggle and death signaled an end, a death to old perspectives, old presuppositions, old practices and old preaching in Christianity. A new way must be shaped out of the ashes of Bonhoeffer and in light of the devastation of the Holocaust.

In a letter from prison entitled "Thoughts on the Day of the Baptism of Dietrich Wilhelm Rudiger Bethge," Bonhoeffer writes,

> Our church, which has been fighting in these years, only for its self-preservation, as though that were an end in itself, is incapable of taking the word of reconciliation and redemption to mankind and the world. Our earlier words are therefore bound to lose their force and cease, and our being Christians today will be limited to two things: prayer and righteous action among men. . . . By the time you have grown up, the church's form will have changed greatly. We are not yet out of the melting-pot, and any attempt to help the church prematurely to a new expansion of its organization will merely delay its conversion and purification.[9]

Fifty years after the end of the Holocaust, churches are still not responding to the need for an examination of anti-Semitic religious education and the need for a reinterpretation of so many scriptures within the New Testament. Just as the Church of Germany failed to see what was happening right under its eyes, the American Church is failing to recognize the significance of that awful tragedy that occurred in the midst of a Christian society.

NOTES

1. Robert McAfee Brown, *Elie Wiesel: Messenger to all Humanity* (Notre Dame: University of Notre Dame Press, 1989), 164.

2. Christopher M. Leighton, Prologue to *Mature Christianity in the 21st Century* by Norman A. Beck (New York: Crossroad, 1994), 50.

3. Norman A. Beck, *Mature Christianity in the 21st Century* (New York: Crossroad, 1994), 82–83.

4. Eberhard Bethge, *Dietrich Bonhoeffer* (New York: Harper & Row, 1985), 511–512.

5. Johann Baptist Metz, *The Emergent Church* (New York: Crossroad, 1981), 22.

6. Brown, op. cit., 47.

7. Ibid., 48

8. Beck, op. cit., 68.

9. Dietrich Bonhoeffer, *Letters and Papers from Prison* (New York: Macmillan, 1971), 300.

CHAPTER 7

THREE AGONIZING QUESTIONS

There are three questions which torment me daily here in this prison, questions for which there are no simple theological answers or resolutions. The first question: Where is God in all of this—when it appears that might does indeed make right, when millions of people are being persecuted and murdered, and when the most insidious and pernicious forms of evil are made to look like piety? I ask myself quite often where is God in the midst of this insanity that has afflicted our nation and our world?

The second question: Who are God's people after all? Some may say that it is the Jews who are God's people. If you assert that it is the Jews who are God's people, I have a question for you. Why is it then that when so many of His people are being murdered, it appears that God is folding his arms in apathy? You may ask how I could say that, being a pastor and a theologian, and you may think I should know that it is Christians who are God's people. If you maintain that it is Christians who are God's people, I have a question for you. Tell me then, why is it that so many of those who usher little children into gas chambers call themselves Christians? Are we God's people?

The third question: Who am I? Am I who they think I am, or who I know myself to be—one who is not at all confident or cheerful, one who is quite often, in fact, desperately depressed and hopeless? Who am I? Oh God, whoever I am, thou knowest I am thine.

N REALITY, THERE EXISTS A record that Dietrich Bonhoeffer asked one of those questions, the question "Who am I?" It is logical, however, to assume that prisoner Bonhoeffer would have voiced both of the other two questions during his two-year imprisonment by the Nazis. One can understand that both the circumstances of his life as a prisoner and the conditions of his homeland would have provoked serious and troubling questions for this pastor and theologian.

Let us address the first question: "*Where is God in all of this?*" I was inspired to inject this question into the play as a result of my mother's suicide in March of 1978. For months prior to her death, our family sought psychological help for her from numerous sources—counseling, hospitalization, group therapy, and anti-depressants. Mother even underwent the controversial electroshock therapy to relieve her deep depression. Nothing seemed to be able to turn her away from the intense desire to relieve her darkness through self-annihilation. My mother was the most dedicated Christian I had ever known. She was the person who most influenced me to consider becoming a minister. Yet, in her last days she doubted her own relationship to God as she told me, "Alfred, I'm not sure that I'm saved." My reply to her was, "Mother, if you are not saved, then no one is." Especially in view of the fact that I had been praying for Mother daily, I wondered "Where is God in of all of this?" It just seemed as though my dear mother had slipped through the cracks and gotten away from us, forsaken by God. The darkness of her depression had defeated her and had defeated all of the family.

I remember my brother's response to the news of my mother's suicide. Without even giving the words a second thought, Tom exclaimed, "This time, God, you made a mistake!" That statement seemed to sum up how all of us felt in the face of this tragedy. I admit that I was filled with anger and even rage at God for what appeared to be His apathy and silence regarding my mother's suffering. One might discount that anger and say it was a faulty response based upon a flawed view of God and of reality. While that may be true, I nevertheless experience tremendous frustration with God in moments of my own distress and the suffering of those dearest to me.

During the time when my first wife, Vicki, was undergoing chemotherapy for cancer, I recall a number of occasions upon which I experienced feelings of anger at God for allowing her suffering. I would usually think back to my mother's pain and depression, and all of the hostility at what I felt was God's passivity would come to the surface in my prayers to God. The prayers typically took the form of "Why, if you are all-powerful, do you not relieve the pain? Why must you remain passive and apathetical in the face of suffering?"

A number of years ago, it seemed that nearly every other automobile in Texas sported a bumper sticker that read "Jesus is the Answer." Someone then designed another one that read "If Jesus is the Answer, what is the Question?" How is Jesus the answer? How is Jesus the answer to the tragic death of children? How is Jesus the answer to the murder of a thirty-year-old businessman who is months away from his wedding day? How is Jesus the answer to a young woman of thirty, the mother of three small children, who has just learned that she has acute leukemia and probably has only months to live? How is Jesus the answer to a teenage girl who has been sexually abused and beaten by her stepfather over a period of ten years? How is Jesus the answer to a young man of twenty-five who is dying of AIDS? How is Jesus the answer to the millions of children who have been orphaned by wars the world over? How is Jesus the answer to a young mother of two whose Navy pilot husband has just been tragically killed in a training exercise crash? How is Jesus the answer to a suicidal teenager who was raped and encouraged by her parents to have an abortion? How is Jesus the answer to a woman who has suffered a mastectomy and then had to undergo the further trauma of her husband leaving her with several small children and the debts?

Where is God in all of this? As a pastor and chaplain, I have heard this question posed many times when patients or families have experienced devastating illnesses, accidents and deaths. I have encountered numerous situations for which there are no easy answers, no band-aid solutions.

In the midst of my grief following my mother's suicide, I reflected upon the scene of the crucifixion of Jesus, who cried out, "My God, my God, why have you forsaken me?" during those terrible hours of agony on the cross and persecution by the soldiers and the crowd of onlookers. I came to realize that as Jesus himself questioned God's seeming passivity during his time of deepest anguish, *it is not a sign of faithlessness* for the rest of us to find ourselves asking, "*Where is God in all of this?*"

Following my presentation of the Bonhoeffer play for a Jewish federation in the Northeast several years ago, I had a conversation with two of the members of the audience who had inquiries about the play. One of the men who talked to me was a Holocaust survivor. I asked him how the experiences in the concentration camps affected his sense of faith, and he responded that it was difficult to pray to God or to believe in God following his experiences as a prisoner. He said, "I saw little babies torn apart by human hands and then I saw their heads bashed up against walls. They would be thrown out of windows and used for target practice by the German soldiers. What kind of God would allow that?"

The other man was a physician whose father was a survivor of one of the many death camps. This young man was struck by the question, "Where is God in all of this?" The physician asked me if Bonhoeffer posed this question or if it was my own creation. I confessed to him that the question was my own, though I did believe that Bonhoeffer must have pondered this question during his time in prison. The Jewish doctor told me that his father could no longer believe in God after what happened to him in the concentration camp.

Elie Wiesel, noted author and Auschwitz survivor, wrestled with this question as he pondered the place of God and the power of God in the midst of so much Jewish suffering and death during the years of the Third Reich. Wiesel's posture resulted in a "theology of protest" that dares to ask where God's power and love were during the years of the Final Solution.

Wiesel speaks of the silence of both God and the bystanders in his writings. In one of his works Wiesel gives us this picture of God. He states that God "watched us depart for the unknown," one "who observed us, without emotion, while we became objects—living sticks of wood—and carefully numbered victims."[1] Wiesel confesses his never-ending struggle with God by saying, "I will never cease to rebel against those who committed or permitted Auschwitz, including God."[2]

In Wiesel's most noted work, entitled *Night*, he tells us of a young boy's death from being hanged on the gallows by the Nazis in front of the other prisoners within the concentration camp. Wiesel says that the boy's death was not immediate because he was light in weight. The prisoners were therefore put through the hell of watching, for what must have seemed like an eternity, the little boy's body struggle with death and finally succumb. One of the prisoners was heard to mutter, "Where is God now?" Another prisoner answered, "He is on the gallows."[3] In commenting upon this oft-cited passage, Wiesel writes the following:

> Theorists of the idea that "God is dead" have used my words unfairly as justification of their rejection of faith . . . I have never renounced my faith in God. I have risen against His justice, protested His silence and sometimes His absence, but my anger rises within faith and not outside it . . . Abraham and Moses, Jeremiah and Rebbe Levi-Yitzhak of Berdichev teach us that it is permissible for man to accuse God, provided it be done in the name of faith in God. If that hurts, so be it. Sometimes we must accept the pain of faith so as not to lose it. . . . As I have said elsewhere, Auschwitz is conceivable neither with God nor without Him. Perhaps I may someday come to understand man's role in the mystery Auschwitz represents, but never God's.[4]

The horrors of the Holocaust pose a serious challenge to so many of the glib platitudes that continue to be pronounced from pulpits and in the Sunday School classrooms of our churches. As Irving Greenberg has said, "Everything we now say about God must make sense in the face of burning children." Wiesel seems to say that the agony of the believer is not whether

God exists. It is that God exists . . . and remains silent. In *Generation* Wiesel poses this dilemma:

> Why and how survive in a universe which negates you? Or: How can you reconcile yourself with history and the graves it digs and transcends? Or: How should you answer the Jewish child who insists: I don't want to suffer, I no longer want to suffer without knowing why. Worse: How does one answer that child's father who says: I don't want, I no longer want, my son to suffer pain and punishment without knowing that his torment has meaning and will have an end? And then, the big question, the most serious of all: How does one answer the person who demands an interpretation of God's silence at the very moment when man—any man, Jew or non-Jew—has greater need than ever of His word, let alone His mercy?[5]

Johann Baptist Metz assails Christianity with having "an excess of answers and a corresponding lack of agonized questions."[6] Wiesel has said on numerous occasions, "I do not have any answers, but I have some very good questions."[7] Most of us who grew up attending Sunday School remember that if a question was posed at the beginning of a class time, that question would almost certainly have to be answered and resolved by the end of that class session. We could not just let the question remain unanswered. There is so much in life and so much in our faith, however, that cannot be answered. It was Thomas Merton who said, "There are so many people running around with their 'answers,' trying to impose them on everybody."[8] For all of those people who would contend that they had a word or an answer from the Lord, Merton said, "Those who are the loudest to affirm they hear Him are people not to be trusted."[9] Certainly, one of the dominant unanswered questions that comes to mind in times of tragedy, trial and adversity is "Where is God in all of this?"

Big Questions

The cries of the children
of Auschwitz, Treblinka,
beg for an answer,
as do the shrieks
of little ones raised
in abusive homes
throughout the world.
Too many young wives suffer
abuse and murder because they
have no rights in their cultures
I sit in my chair of ease and do not hear;
yet even the silence of my tranquil state
is troubled by what I cannot hear and
what I have not heard,
before my time and in my time.

Where is God?
Where is the Father of this creation
that moans under the weight of being
consigned to powerlessness and pain,
to pitiable existence?
Words, answers, doctrines
do not offer solace to tragic lives,
and most especially since the words flow
from mouths far removed from the
contexts of horror.

O answer-giver,
have you sat helpless beneath a barrage
of violent strokes against your face and back
and suffered the withering and vile verbal torture
that shreds the body and the spirit?
How does one understand
the rightness of creation in all this misery?
If anyone should provide the answer,

it is the sufferer, not the observer.
To be honest, we must concede
that there are no answers,
only questions,
as many as the afflictions and abuses
that continue unabated, unhindered.
Perhaps judgment will not only entail
the accounting of the sins of humanity,
but will also include the countless
questions addressed to the Creator:
Why?
Where were you?
Why did we suffer?
Why were there no intercessions?
Why have our questions had to wait
thousands of years?

Metz states in a compelling manner his impressions of what Auschwitz means to his identity as a Christian. He says, "Faced with Auschwitz, I consider as blasphemy every Christian theodicy (i.e., every attempt at a so-called "justification of God") and all language about 'meaning' when these are initiated outside this catastrophe or on some level above it."[10] Metz seems to take Auschwitz as the centerpiece of a new theological posture for Christians. He adds, "After Auschwitz, every theological 'profundity' which is unrelated to people and their concrete situations must cease to exist. Such a theology would be the very essence of superficiality." Metz' words sound very much like those of Wiesel, who says, "Any view of the present that fails to acknowledge that there was a Holocaust in the past, threatens the future."[11]

Theologian David Blumenthal makes a convincing argument for a "theology of protest" in his book *Facing the Abusing God: A Theology of Protest*. Blumenthal states that "The theology of protest goes back to the Bible and is present forcefully in the Book of Job."[12] He continues, "Job never questions God's existence, nor God's power to do what God is doing. Rather, Job questions God's justification, God's morality, God's justice. Throughout, Job rejects the moral panaceas and the theological rationalizations of his friends, as does God in the end. No pat answer; rather, the repeated assertion of his innocence and the recurrent questioning of God's justice. No easy resolutions; rather, the repeated assertion of loyalty of God and the recurrent accusation of injustice."[13]

What many preachers have done in interpreting Job is point to the fact that Job was much better off in the latter part of his life, that God vindicated him by restoring his health and his fortune. How can the death of one's children ever be made right? To lose a child is to live with a dagger in one's heart for the remainder of a parent's life.

During my pastorate in Portales, New Mexico, I met a couple, with two small children, who had suffered a great tragedy a few years earlier. They had lost three young daughters and the wife's parents. The grandparents had been babysitting the three little girls while their parents were away, and all five of them were killed by a horrific blast from a gas leak in the grandparents' home late one evening. As I would visit the family, I knew that even though these young parents were thrilled about the birth of their two recent babies, they would always carry an awful, aching grief over the loss of their first three children.

In his text on Job, Stephen Mitchell says that the new children of Job at the end of Job's trials are in fact the old children. He writes, "He (Job) is given seven sons and three daughters, as before, all of them instantaneously grown up; they have sprung back to life as gracefully as the bones of a murdered child in a Grimms' tale." Certainly this interpretation would make the account of the later life of Job and his wife more palatable than the assumption that Job and his wife forgot the anguish of losing their children simply because they had more children later in life.

Now for the second question: *"Who are God's people after all?"* Baptists, indeed Christians of all denominations, would contend that the acceptance of Jesus Christ as Savior alone qualifies people as God's people. According to Baptist belief and conservative Christian belief, those who do not accept Jesus as their Savior are not children of God in the truest sense. This view was conveyed on a very public forum by then Southern Baptist Convention President Bailey Smith in 1981. Speaking to a large gathering, Smith proclaimed, "It's interesting at great political rallies, how you have a Protestant to pray, a Catholic to pray and then you have a Jew to pray. With all due respect to those dear people, my friends, God Almighty does not hear the prayer of a Jew. For how in the world can God hear the prayer of a man who says that Jesus Christ is not the true Messiah? That is blasphemy."

A real dilemma rears its head, of course, as one reflects on the manner in which "God's children," Christians, have treated Jews for centuries. Elie Wiesel says in this regard, "Any messiah in whose name men are tortured can only be a false messiah."[14] Wiesel's indictments against Christians, and they are more than deserved, are many. In another stinging criticism of Christianity, Wiesel says, "If you study the history of Christianity you will see that it is full of anti-Semitism.[15] More than that—there would have been no Auschwitz if the way had not been prepared by Christian theology. Among the first to dehumanize the Jew was the Christian . . ."[16]

The Holocaust brought out into the open the ugly germ

of anti-Semitism that has been a part of Christian theology, education and preaching since the inception of Christianity. The anti-Semitic attitudes that paved the way for the Shoah did not just appear for the first time during the 1930s. These attitudes and views had been prominent for generations. Consider the Reformer Martin Luther and his statements about the Jews:

> What then shall we do with this damned rejected race of Jews? Since they live among us and we know about their lying and blasphemy and cursing, we cannot tolerate them if we do not wish to share in their lies, curses, and blasphemy. In this way we cannot quench the inextinguishable fire of divine rage (as the prophets say) nor convert the Jews. We must prayerfully and reverently practice a merciful severity. Perhaps we may save a few from the fire and the flames. They are surely being punished a thousand times more than we might wish them. Let me give you my honest advice.
>
> First, their synagogues or churches should be set on fire, and whatever does not burn up should be covered or spread with dirt so that no one may ever be able to see a cinder or stone of it. And this ought to be done for the honour of God and of Christianity in order that God may see that we are Christians, and that we have not wittingly tolerated or approved of such public lying, cursing and blaspheming of His Son and His Christians . . .
>
> Secondly, their homes should likewise be broken down and destroyed. For they perpetuate the same things there that they do in their synagogues. For the same reason they ought to be put under one roof or in a stable, like gypsies, in order that they may realize that they are not masters in our land, as they boast, but miserable captives, as they complain of us incessantly before God with bitter wailing.
>
> Thirdly, they should be deprived of their prayer-books and Talmuds in which such idolatry, lies, cursing, and blasphemy are taught.
>
> Fourthly, their rabbis must be forbidden under threat of death to teach any more . . .

Fifthly, passport and traveling privileges must be absolutely forbidden to the Jews. For they have no business in the rural districts, since they are not nobles, nor officials, nor merchants, nor the like . . .

Sixthly, they ought to be stopped from usury. All their cash and valuables of silver and gold ought to be taken from them and put aside for safe keeping. For this reason, as said before, everything that they possess they stole and robbed from us through their usury, for they have no other means of support. . . . Such evilly acquired money is cursed, unless, with God's blessing, it is put to some good and necessary use. . .

Seventhly, let the young and strong Jews and Jewesses be given the flail, the ax, the hoe, the spade, the distaff, and spindle, and let them earn their bread by the sweat of their noses as is enjoined upon Adam's children. For it is not proper that they should want us cursed Goyim to work in the sweat of our brow and that they, pious crew, while away their days at the fireside in idleness, feasting and display. And in addition to this, they boast impiously that they have become masters of the Christians at their expense. We ought to drive the rascally lazy bones out of our system. If however we are afraid that they might harm us personally . . . then let us apply the same cleverness as the other nations, such as France, Spain, Bohemia, etc., and settle with them for that which they have extorted usuriously from us, and after having divided it up fairly let us drive them out of the country for all time. For, as has been said, God's rage is so great against them that they only become worse and worse through mild mercy, and not much better through severe mercy. Therefore away with them . . .[17]

As author William Nicholls notes, "At his trial in Nuremberg after the Second World War, Julius Streicher, the notorious Nazi propagandist, editor of the scurrilous anti-Semitic weekly, *Der Sturmer*, argued that if he should be standing there arraigned on such charges, so should Martin Luther."[18] Luther, who had been so tolerant of Jews early in his career, espouses still a more hateful diatribe against the Jews by saying, "We are at fault in not avenging all this innocent blood of our Lord and of the Christians which they shed for three hundred years after the destruction of Jerusalem, and the blood of children they have shed since then (which still shines forth from their eyes and their skin). *We are at fault in not slaying them.*[19] Luther's views of Jews were deadly in their import, for the Nazis were quite willing to resurrect Luther's ghastly pamphlet for use in their propaganda.

John Chrysostom has been called the greatest preacher in all Christian history. Yet even Chrysostom wrote, "Jews fought against the commands of God and danced with the Devil." Among the other diatribes against Jews, Chrysostom added, "It was not by their own power that the Caesars did what they did to you (Jews); it was done by the wrath of God, and his absolute rejection of you."[20] Finally, in a work entitled *Against the Jews*, Chrysostom writes, "Although such beasts (Jews) are unfit for work, they are fit for killing. And this is what happened to the Jews: while they were making themselves unfit for work, they grew fit for slaughter."[21] The attitudes of Luther and Chrysostom are in concert with the sympathies of Hitler himself who said, "I believe that I am acting in accordance with the will of the Almighty Creator: by defending myself against the Jew, I am fighting for the work of the Lord."[22]

Who are God's people? Are the chosen people the Jews? The Holocaust raises this question for both Jew and Christian. For the Jew, the question must be that "If we are your children, why were so many of us murdered without your intervention?" On the eve of the Six Day War, Wiesel pours out his frustration over the silence of God during the devastation of the Shoah and says,

I cannot go on. If this time again You desert Your people, if this

time again You permit the slaughterer to murder Your children
and besmirch their allegiance to the covenant, if this time You
let Your promise become mockery, then know, O Master of all
that breathes, know that You no longer deserve Your people's
love and their passion to sanctify You, to justify You toward and
against all, toward and against Yourself; if this time again the
survivors are massacred and their deaths held up to ridicule . . .
before dying I shall shout as no victim has ever shouted, and
know that each of my tears and each of my shouts will tarnish
your glory, each of my gestures will negate You and will negate
me as You have negated me. . . ."[23]

In consideration of the question as to whether Christians
are "God's People" we must consider a significant problem that
the Holocaust raises for Christians. The question is posed by
Robert McAfee Brown as he says that the problem is "the problem of complicity, the problem of why so many Christians laid
the historical groundwork for the anti-Semitism that flowered
under Hitler, and were either active proponents of Hitler's policies, or stayed on the sidelines playing the role of spectator."[24]
Wiesel once remarked that "The Christians betrayed the Christ
more than the Jews did."[25]

Brown cites what he believes is the most significant statement from any church organization on the place of Jews and
Christians. The document is from the Synod of the Protestant
Church of the Rhineland, issued on January 11, 1980. The statement includes these insights: "(1) recognition of Christian co-
responsibility and guilt in the Holocaust: the defamation,
persecution and murder of the Jews in the Third Reich; (2) new
biblical insights regarding the enduring significance of Israel in
redemption history (e.g., Rom. 9–11) which were obtained as
a result of the Church Struggle; (3) the insight that the continuing existence of the Jewish people, its return to the land of
promise and the creation of the State of Israel are signs of God's

faithfulness to his people; (4) the willingness of Jews to meet, engage in joint study and work in spite of the Holocaust."[26] As a result of this organization's conclusions, the Synod goes on to state, "We confess with sorrow the co-responsibility and guilt of Christianity in Germany with respect to the Holocaust." The statement further says, "[W]e believe in the continuing election of the Jewish people as the people of God and recognize that through Jesus Christ, the Church has been included in the covenant of God with his people . . . (we) reject the view that the people of Israel is rejected of God or displaced by the church. . . ."[27]

The previous statement should have been placed in the sanctuary of every church within the United States. Such a statement would call into question any attempt by Christians to evangelize the Jewish people. In 1999 the Southern Baptist Convention managed to once again offend the Jewish people of our nation by releasing "prayer guides" during the High Holy Days of the Jewish faith. Needless to say, these prayer guides set off an enormous protest within the Jewish community and considerable protest within the life of the church.

Robert McAfee Brown provides insight to Baptists and other Christian communities on the subject of evangelization of Jews through this assertion:

> The history of the Christian church is so baleful in relation to the Jews that there is an arrogance and insensitivity almost beyond comprehension in the Christian assumption that somehow Jews "need" to be part of that community, or would even feel welcome or fulfilled in the body that has destroyed so many tens of thousands of Jews in the past . . . If a Jew wishes to become a Christian, that is, of course, a decision he or she must be free to make, and the Christian community is graced by such presence, but the initiative belongs with the Jew rather than the Christian.[28]

Regarding the subject of evangelization, the first order of business for the Christian church is to allow the spirit of evangelization, of conversion to penetrate into the lives of every Christian. This conversion would manifest itself in a radical change in attitudes, doctrines and relationships toward the Jewish community of faith. Conversion begins with a conviction of the need for repentance. The Church needs to undergo repentance for her own sins of hate-mongering toward Jews and for her apathy toward the plight of Jews throughout the history of the Church. William Nicholls explains the importance of this spirit of repentance within the Church as follows:

> The Holocaust cannot be undone, nor the six million brought back from the ashes of the crematoria. Only the dead have the right to forgive, and no one, least of all Christians, has the right to forgive on their behalf. Nevertheless, some theologians now believe that repentance for the anti-Semitism that betrayed Jesus and inflicted unimaginable harm on his people is a spiritual necessity for Christians themselves, whether or not it can earn forgiveness from Jews. Such repentance, if real, cannot fail to lead to theological change.[29]

NOTES

1. Robert McAfee Brown, *Elie Wiesel: Messenger to all Humanity* (Notre Dame: University of Notre Dame Press, 1989): 74.

2. Elie Wiesel, *Memoirs: All Rivers Run to the Sea* (New York: Schocken, 1995), 72.

3. Brown, op. cit., 55–56.

4. Wiesel, op. cit., 84.

5. Brown, op.cit., 144.

6. Johann Baptist Metz, *The Emergent Church* (New York: Crossroad, 1981), 23.

7. Elie Wiesel, *The Trial of God* (New York: Schocken, 1979), xvi.

8. Thomas Merton, *Witness to Freedom*. Ed. by William H. Shannon (New York: Harcourt Brace & Company, 1994), 339.

9. Ibid., 329.

10. Metz, op.cit., 19.

11. Brown, op. cit., 204.

12. David R. Blumenthal, *Facing the Abusing God: A Theology of Protest* (Louisville KY: Westminster/John Knox Press, 1993), 250–51.

13. Ibid., 251.

14. Brown, op. cit., 174.

15. Ibid., 170–71.

16. William Nicholls, *Christian Antisemitism: A History of Hate* (Northvale: Jason Aronson, 1995), 270–71.

17. Ibid., 271.

18. Christopher M. Leighton, Prologue to *Mature Christianity in the 21st Century* by Norman A. Beck (New York: Crossroad, 1994), 22.

19. Marvin Perry and Frederick M. Schweitzer, Eds. *Jewish-Christian Encounters over the Centuries* (New York: Peter Lang, 1994), 114.

20. Ibid., 114.

21. Leighton, op. cit., 22.

22. Ibid., 22.

23. Brown, op. cit., 149–50.

24. Ibid., 170.

25. Ibid., 173.

26. Ibid., 178.

27. Ibid., 179.

28. Ibid., 187.

29. Nicholls, op. cit., xxviii.

CHAPTER 8

RACISM AND THE UNDERSIDE OF HISTORY

Whenever I begin to reflect and remember, I usually begin with the years 1930 and 1931, when I attended Union Theological Seminary in New York City. There I had the opportunity to study with America's preeminent theologian, Reinhold Niebuhr. And as important as Professor Niebuhr's influence was upon my young life, there was one other person during that time who was to have an equal impact upon me. That was the person of Frank Fisher, a black man. It was Fisher who introduced me to the hidden side of this nation that was so proud of her piety. It was Fisher who introduced me to Harlem. He introduced me to racism. And it was through my association with Frank Fisher and through worshipping at his church, the Abyssinian Baptist Church, there in the middle of Harlem, that I came to the most profound and radical revelation of my entire life. Here it is, quite simply: For the first time in my privileged existence, I began to look at life, history and the interpretation of scripture from a totally different perspective, from the perspective of the outcasts, the reviled, the suspects, the prisoners, the marginalized, the oppressed, the poor. In short, I began to look at all of these from the perspective of all who suffer!

I T SHOULD BE NO SURPRISE THAT, during the year he lived and studied in New York, Bonhoeffer identified with the poverty of the African-American community in Harlem. It was during that year that young Bonhoeffer began to understand the connection between extreme poverty and the institution of racism. One of Bonhoeffer's closest friends during that year was Frank Fisher, a fellow student at Union Theological Seminary. Dietrich Bonhoeffer called his friendship with the African-American community of Abyssinian Baptist Church and Harlem "one of the most decisive and delightful happenings of my stay in America." Geffrey Kelly helps us to understand the import of Bonhoeffer's relationship with the African-American community in Harlem by observing:

> But, while he admired the deep spirituality of their liturgical hymns, Bonhoeffer also noticed the impatience of young African-Americans at their elders' stoically enduring injustice in a country that bragged of its love of freedom. He believed

strongly that, if these young people were ever to become godless because of the rampant racism they encountered and the absence of any real church support on their behalf, "white America would have to acknowledge its guilt."[1]

Bonhoeffer introduced his Finkenwalde students to the Negro spiritual and told them of the statement made to him by Frank Fisher just prior to Bonhoeffer's return to Germany in 1931. Fisher said, "Make our sufferings known in Germany, tell them what is happening to us, and show them what we are like."[2] Kelly writes, "Having absorbed from Fisher a sensitivity to the economic misery of America's blacks, and having tracked their woes not only to racism but also to ecclesiastical apathy, Bonhoeffer was doubly alert to the menace of Hitler's racist ideology. He recognized that in the laws then being concocted to deny the Jewish citizens their fundamental human rights, a contemptuous gauntlet was being thrown down at the churches."[3]

Eberhard Bethge states that "Bonhoeffer regards the characteristics of religion . . . as failing to recognize not only the presence, but also the person of Jesus."[4] One of those characteristics that Bethge enumerates is that "He (Jesus) turns away from the privileged classes and sits down with the outcasts."[5] As a young German theologian-pastor, Bonhoeffer had enjoyed the privileges of education, culture and notable family connections because of his family's status in German society. He seemed to be extremely sensitive to the fact that his life had been made easier by virtue of his family's social standing. His life of advocacy and service to those less fortunate is reminiscent of the story of Albert Schweitzer. Because of the advantages that he had enjoyed in pursuing doctorates in several fields, Dr. Schweitzer felt a particular obligation to utilize that knowledge and skill in the service of those less fortunate.

The biblical motif of this "downwardly mobile" lifestyle

can be seen in the story of Moses, who abdicated his powerful role in the Egyptian government to take up the cause of the oppressed children of Israel. The tribute to Moses in the Roll Call of Faith is found in Hebrews 11:24–26:

> By faith Moses, when he had grown up, refused to be known as the son of Pharaoh's daughter. He chose to be mistreated along with the people of God rather than to enjoy the pleasures of sin for a short time. He regarded disgrace for the sake of Christ as of greater value than the treasures of Egypt, because he was looking ahead to his reward.

Those who follow the pattern of Jesus are given this advice in Philippians 2:5–8:

> Your attitude should be the same as that of Christ Jesus: who, being in very nature God, did not consider equality with God something to be grasped, but made himself nothing, taking the very nature of a servant, being made in human likeness. And being found in appearance as a man, he humbled himself and became obedient to death—even death on a cross!

This lifestyle motif sharply contrasts with the American way of life that honors and glorifies the "upwardly mobile." Americans use various terms, such as "getting ahead," "climbing the ladder" and "getting to the top" to signify the direction of our career and lifestyle goals.

Moving Up

What are the payments on a BMW?
What kind of work does one do to manage a Mercedes?
Random thoughts while jogging on the north side of town.
How do these people vote?
Does one really need to ask?
"Ditto Rush" signs on their bumpers.
Where do they go to church?

And what do their preachers say to them Sunday by Sunday?

We're getting ready for another banner year for Republicans
and the right-wing evangelical Christians.
(Well, that's redundant, we all know.)
The preachers are energizing their flocks
and their viewers and listeners,
reminding us to get out the vote
and to remember what made this country great.
Tell us again, boys, the "whole story."
That's the bad thing about some kinds of religion—
a lot of truth is left out.

That's what bothers me while jogging on the north side of town.
So many ministers standing in pulpits
not talking about all of the issues.
"Well, as long as you keep holding up Jesus,
that's all that matters."
REALLY?

Nothing is as bad as religion that disguises itself as
TRUTH, as THE truth from God,
the indisputable, the inarguable.
Lately, though, that word has started to become abusive
like the master beating his slave
while reading his Bible.
God and Jesus have been tucked into
the pocket of a political party.

O holy men clothed with arrogance and power,
let me urge you to tackle the prophets again.
Go to the real school of the Prophets and discover
what NEW word these troublesome
troubadours might say to you—
that religion as a form doesn't mean a hill of dung—
that praising and preaching and praying
are pure nonsense without JUSTICE.
Reread that, preacher man, in your

floppy red King James or Living Bible.
It's all going to say the same—that
JUSTICE EQUALS RIGHTEOUSNESS.

In my various associations with college students over the years, I have observed that the typical evangelical college student does not appear to possess an awareness of the harsh realities that the underprivileged of our nation have to contend with every single day of their lives. It is difficult to find students in church-related schools who are conversant about the ever-widening gap between the rich and the poor in this nation and the import of that phenomenon for Christians. During my two decades of service as a college minister and later as a college speaker and lecturer, I have met very few college students who display a social conscience or awareness of the social and political implications of the teachings of the prophets and the teachings of Jesus. A vast majority of students appear to parrot the values of the society in which they were raised—a very materialistic, compartmentalized Christianity which devotes most of its energy to window-dressing morality such as prayer in schools and the necessity of having prayer before football games and at graduations.

Where are the social passion and the spirit of advocacy that characterized my generation, the generation of the '60s? Admittedly, my generation was misguided about many issues, as well as the way to carry out the needed reforms of society. Our generation did possess a social conscience, however, and a social passion that could look beyond our own class, our own color, religion and gender. This is what I see missing in so many young people who attend Christian youth rallies, revivals and concerts. One is also not likely to hear Christian leaders, pastors or evangelists encouraging their hearers to give their lives in service to the poor and underprivileged. No, what is almost exclusively emphasized is an inward ethic, a life devoid of real advocacy, a life that has no "witness" for those less privileged. Sometimes I think these massive displays of youthful spirituality are giant exercises in blasphemy, for the systemic evils of injustice and greed are never talked about, they are never addressed.

The new perspective of the "view from below" that Bonhoeffer reached early in his career was a concept that would later be appropriated by liberation theologians of the 1960s and '70s. None other than Gustavo Gutierrez called Bonhoeffer a "seminal liberationist," thus attributing to this German pastor the principle that would evoke such a wave of change in Latin America and in Africa and among African-Americans and women in the United States. Dietrich Bonhoeffer did not need to look to developing trends of thought to understand this principle of God's special concern for the oppressed. This concept of "God's Preferential Option for the Poor" is a fundamental teaching in both the Hebrew and Christian scriptures. The following scriptures are some of the most prominent teachings that could have greatly influenced Bonhoeffer's "view from below:"

"Why have we fasted," they say, "and you have not seen it? Why have we humbled ourselves, and you have not noticed?"

Yet on the day of your fasting, you do as you please and exploit all your workers.

Your fasting ends in quarreling and strife, and in striking each other with wicked fists.

You cannot fast as you do today and expect your voice to be heard on high.

Is this the kind of fast I have chosen, only a day for a man to humble himself?

Is it only for bowing one's head like a reed and for lying on sackcloth and ashes?

Is that what you call a fast, a day acceptable to the Lord?

Is this not the kind of fasting I have chosen: to loose the chains of injustice and untie the cord of the yoke, to set the oppressed free and break every yoke?

Is it not to share your food with the hungry and to provide the poor wanderer with shelter - when you see the naked, to clothe him, and not to turn away from your own flesh and blood?

Then your light will break forth like the dawn, and your healing will quickly appear; then your righteousness will go before you, and the glory of the Lord will be your rear guard.

Then you will call, and the Lord will answer; you will cry for help, and he will say: Here am I.

If you do away with the yoke of oppression, with the pointing finger and malicious talk, and if you spend yourselves in behalf of the hungry and satisfy the needs of the oppressed, then your light will rise in the darkness, and your night will become like the noonday.

— Isaiah 58:3–10

Woe to him who builds his palace by unrighteousness, his upper rooms by injustice, making his countrymen work for nothing, not paying them for their labor.

He says, "I will build myself a great palace with spacious upper rooms."

So he makes large windows in it, panels it with cedar and decorates it in red.

Does it make you a king to have more and more cedar?

Did not your father have food and drink?

He did what was right and just, so all went well with him.

He defended the cause of the poor and needy, and so all went well.

Is that not what it means to know me? declares the Lord.

But your eyes and your heart are set only on dishonest gain, on shedding innocent blood and on oppression and extortion.

— Jeremiah 22: 13–17

I hate, I despise your religious feasts; I cannot stand your assemblies.

Even though you bring me burnt offerings and grain offerings, I will not accept them.

Though you bring choice fellowship offerings, I will have no regard for them.

Away with the noise of your songs! I will not listen to the music of your harps.

But let justice roll on like a river, righteousness like a never-failing stream!

— Amos 5:21–24

With what shall I come before the Lord and bow down before the exalted God?

Shall I come before him with burnt offerings, with calves a year old?

Will the Lord be pleased with thousands of rams, with ten thousand rivers of oil?

Shall I offer my firstborn for my transgression, the fruit of my body for the sin of my soul?

He has showed you, O man, what is good.

And what does the Lord require of you?

To act justly and to love mercy and to walk humbly with your God.

— Micah 6:6–8

When the Son of Man comes in his glory, and all the angels with him, he will sit on his throne in heavenly glory. All the nations will be gathered before him, and he will separate the people one from another as a shepherd separates the sheep from the goats. He will put the sheep on his right and the goats on his left.

Then the King will say to those on his right, "Come, you who are blessed by my Father; take your inheritance, the kingdom prepared for you since the creation of the world. For I was hungry and you gave me something to eat, I was thirsty and you gave me something to drink, I was a stranger and you invited me in, I needed clothes and you clothed me, I was sick and you looked after me, I was in prison and you came to visit me."

Then the righteous will answer him, "Lord, when did we see you hungry and feed you, or thirsty and give you something to drink? When did we see you a stranger and invite you in, or needing clothes and clothe you? When did we see you sick or in prison and go to visit you?"

The King will reply, "I tell you the truth, whatever you did for one of the least of these brothers of mine, you did for me."

Then he will say to those on his left, "Depart from me, you who are cursed, into the eternal fire prepared for the devil and his angels. For I was hungry and you gave me nothing to eat, I was thirsty and you gave me nothing to drink, I was a stranger and you did not invite me in, I needed clothes and you did not clothe me, I was sick and in prison and you did not look after me."

They also will answer, "Lord, when did we see you hungry or thirsty or a stranger or needing clothes or sick or in prison, and did not help you?"

He will reply, "I tell you the truth, whatever you did not do for one of the least of these, you did not do for me."

Then they will go away to eternal punishment, but the righteous to eternal life.

— Matthew 25:31–46

NOTES

1. Geffrey Kelly, "Bonhoeffer and Romero," *Theology and the Practice of Responsibility*. Ed. by Wayne Whitson Floyd Jr. and Charles Marsh (Valley Forge: Trinity Press International, 1994), 87.

2. Ibid., 87.

3. Ibid., 87.

4 Eberhard Bethge, *Dietrich Bonhoeffer* (New York: Harper & Row, 1985), 781.

5 Ibid., 781.

CHAPTER 9

THE DECISION

Shortly after I returned to Germany, I made the decision—to join the conspiracy. Oh, I know what you are thinking: "How could you—a minister, a pastor—align yourself with something as vile, as violent, as unpatriotic as this! Explain this to us, Pastor Bonhoeffer!" I cannot explain or rationalize what was and is and will always be an evil decision. And I would never think of building some kind of systematic ethic based upon what we felt compelled to do. But you must understand this—that we who are Christians in Germany have been thrust on the horns of an ethical dilemma. We cannot escape guilt. Whether we do something or do not do something, we are guilty either way.

Perhaps you have heard of that ethical axiom that "Not to speak is to speak. Likewise, not to act is to act." What that really means and how it translates into the vernacular of everyday life is this: If I am standing in the doorway of my safe and secure little house with my family and I observe a perpetrator on the street persecuting an innocent victim and I say to myself, "Well, the perpetrator is not bothering me and my household, so that is none of my business," that is not true! For with that kind of posture one becomes a facilitator, an accomplice. One becomes complicit with that violence on the street by inaction! It is, for all practical purposes, the sin of omission. As our brother James reminds us in the scriptures, "Sin is to know good and do it not." If there is a madman driving his motorcar on the street running over helpless pedestrians, it is not enough to simply pick up the victims. One must get the madman off the street! Please hear me. Please hear me. Silence is the friend of the perpetrator.

There are three kinds of people in Germany these days, only three. First, there are the Victims. Secondly, there are the Perpetrators. And the third kind? These are the Guilty Bystanders. There are no more classifications!

RECALL MEETING A FORMER PASTOR of the First Baptist Church of Atlanta, Georgia in 1989, while I was pursuing doctoral studies at Southern Baptist Theological Seminary in Louisville. When I mentioned my work with the Bonhoeffer play, the pastor expressed his strong disagreement with Bonhoeffer's decision to become involved in "regicide," the killing of the king. A couple of months ago I encountered another Baptist leader, an area Baptist coordinator, or Associational Director as he is called. He explained to me that although he admired Bonhoeffer's writings and his courage, he nonetheless did not agree with Bonhoeffer's decision to become involved in the conspiracy against Hitler. I also participated in a panel following the performance of my play in Washington State where one of the panelists claimed to be a pacifist. He said because of his belief in pacifism he could not condone Bonhoeffer's decision.

There is no question that Dietrich Bonhoeffer's involvement in the conspiracy was a difficult ethical dilemma. How does a person of faith align involvement in the conspiracy against Hitler with the biblical injunction not to kill? In Bonhoeffer's view, to decide not to become involved in the effort against Hitler would mean complicity with the machinery of death that Hitler had created.

For my own understanding I have had to interpret ethical decisions in light of difficult choices. It is sometimes impossible to live in this world without having to make decisions that involve some sense of guilt either way. For instance, consider the situation in which a woman who has several children is married to an abusive and violent husband. The husband is an alcoholic who daily abuses the wife and children and regularly threatens to kill them while holding a loaded pistol. What is the wife to do in such an awful and dangerous situation? If she decides not to divorce and, therefore, avoid the pain and guilt of going against God's perfect will for the institution of marriage, she subjects herself and her children to further abuse and possibly even murder. On the other hand, she has the choice to divorce, which will save her emotional and physical health and that of her children. There is no "right" way out for this woman. Either decision she makes has ethical consequences. It is my conviction that this is similar to the dilemma Dietrich Bonhoeffer faced in the context of the Third Reich and the reign of Adolf Hitler.

It was Edmund Burke who said, "All it takes for evil to prosper is for good people to do absolutely nothing." The vast majority of German people were silent during the twelve years of the Third Reich. Bonhoeffer came to the conclusion that to remain silent and do nothing would be to align himself with the murderers within the Third Reich. In a section called "Confession Guilt" from his book *Ethics*, Bonhoeffer states, "By her own silence she (the Church) has rendered herself guilty of the decline in responsible action, in bravery in the defense of a cause, and in willingness to suffer for what is known to be right. She bears the guilt of the defection of the governing authority from Christ."[1]

Silence is not always golden. Sometimes it is sinful. How many times I have witnessed numerous well-meaning Christians remaining silent in order to "keep the peace," thus allowing those misguided ones who were more vocal to take charge of organizations, make laws, dictate customs and elect leaders. Such silence is not noble, it is cowardly and it is sinful.

Martin Buber, whose influence can be seen in Wiesel's *The Town Beyond the Wall*, states in *I and Thou* that "Whoever hates directly is closer to a relation than those who are without love and hate." In his commentary on the views of Elie Wiesel, Robert McAfee Brown says, "It is the lack of relationship, indifference, that characterizes the spectator, and it is the most dehumanizing of all human acts, for it destroys both the observer and the one observed."[2] He continues,

> Spectators are without love and also without hate, and this makes the spectator the most morally culpable of all, even more than the executioner. For spectators, unwilling to do the dirty work themselves, consent to letting others do the dirty work on their behalf, encouraging them by silent complicity: "Go ahead. We will watch. And while we will not participate, neither will we condemn. You get our vote by default." So the spectator is not really neutral. The spectator sides with the executioner.[3]

James Russell Lowell wrote,

> They are slaves who fear to speak
> For the fallen and the weak;
> They are slaves who will not choose
> Hatred, scoffing, and abuse,
> Rather than in silence shrink
> From the truth they needs must think;
> They are slaves who dare not be

In the right with two or three.[4]

During the years of the "Irangate" scandal and the efforts of Oliver North to arm the Contras in Nicaragua, his activities were being encouraged by many of the leaders of the Religious Right. I felt the need as a Baptist pastor to focus attention in my sermons on the plight of innocent civilian victims who were being killed and maimed as a result of the work of Lt. Col. North and his operatives. Yet I encountered quite a number of people in my parish who expressed strong opposition to my mentioning these issues from the pulpit. I recall suggesting that our local Baptist association, at its annual meeting, draft a resolution condemning the activities of Lt. Col. North. One retired Air Force Colonel stood up with an air of indignation and stated his opposition to my proposal. Nothing more was said by anyone else. It was simply easier for the others to let the issue be tabled and dropped than to raise any ethical questions and thereby risk some discomfort and possible misunderstandings among our fellowship.

Baptists, especially Southern Baptists, have a long record of silence on difficult ethical issues. Not all Baptists believed in the institutions of slavery, racism and segregation, but because of the silence of those who may have harbored doubts about the rightness of these systemic evils, they continued to exist and even thrive in the South long after voices of conscience began to be raised in the North. The women's issue for most churches is just not talked about, not discussed for fear that bringing the issue to the church floor for open discussion might lead to dissension. So those who continue to occupy powerful pulpits in Southern Baptist life can make their pontifical statements that relegate wives to "submission" and women ministers to being *directors* of youth or *directors* of children's education but never *ministers* of youth or *ministers* of education, and certainly not senior ministers or pastors. The many who will say nothing out of fear of trouble relinquish their views to the pompous powerful, the outspoken elite who occupy conspicuous places of power in Baptist life. Silence is not golden. It is cowardly and it is a refusal to embrace one's responsibility to speak for truth and to speak for those whose rights are deprived.

Apathy

Death by apathy is subtle, very subtle.
Apathy never confronts its victim.
There is no contact between the
apathetical one and the doomed one.
There are no sounds of pain or anguish.

Death by apathy is distant and clean.
Apathy is so impersonal as to not even
take account of its victims.
Apathy vindicates itself through a
maze of self-justifications and rationalizations.
Apathy reduces down to words,
an inundation of verbiage
and seemingly plausible platitudes.
Apathy is void of sensitivity and compassion.
Bullets kill. So does apathy.

NOTES

1. Dietrich Bonhoeffer, *Ethics* (New York: Macmillan, 1986), 115.

2. Robert McAfee Brown, *Elie Wiesel: Messenger to all Humanity* (Notre Dame: University of Notre Dame Press, 1989), 73.

3. Ibid., 73.

4. James Russell Lowell, *The Vision of Sir Launfal and Other Poems* (Boston: Houghton Mifflin, 1905), 23.

CHAPTER 10

HITLER'S SUCCESSFUL PLATFORM

And then there was 1933. Would you explain to me how that could happen? How could a nation that was so technologically advanced, so culturally astute, so "Christian" in her orientation . . . how could that nation allow a maniac such as Adolf Hitler to take control and to maintain control for twelve agonizing years? Well, I have my theories and here they are: First of all, you must understand that Hitler promised a restoration of the national economy. Secondly, he promised to restore respect for Germany among the nations of the world through intense militarization. Thirdly, Hitler promised to vigorously fight the Bolsheviks. Fourthly, he promised to restore "traditional moral values" to German life. Fifthly, he promised us "security." And oh, how we Christians in Germany bowed before the god of Security, while we allowed the systemic evil of genocide to eat at our souls like a cancer. God will not hold us guiltless!

ICHARD PIERARD WRITES THAT "The Protestant press in 1933 was full of editorials affirming that Germany's honor would be vindicated. The humiliation of the lost world war would be left behind. Old moral values of authority, family, home, and church would be restored. The stagnant economy would move once again."[1] In his studies of Southern Baptists' response to Hitler, William Lloyd Allen provides a pertinent quote from Dr. M. E. Dodd, president of the Southern Baptist Convention in 1934:

> Our observation is, that while Hitlerism is doubtless not the ultimate end, for Germany directly or Europe indirectly, it is for Germany a safe step in the right direction. Nazism has at least been a bar to the universal boast of Bolshevism.[2]

Bolshevism, or communism, was the great fear of many Germans during the early 1930s. In the view of most Germans and many Americans in 1933, Nazism and Hitler were far better than the threat of communism. Thus, the foundation for attributing to Bonhoeffer the statement concerning the five reasons for Hitler's ascent to power is well founded in history.

In reviewing the United States political scene of the last twenty years, one can observe amazing parallels to the political platform of Adolf Hitler and the Nazis. The issue of the economy appears to be the most important concern of a majority of Americans. What the majority of Americans seek is a candidate who can promise "a car in every garage." A few years ago it was popular for a presidential candidate to ask, "Are you better off financially than you were four years ago?" Inflation, unemployment, stock prices and the standard of living are the most important concerns to most Americans. Legislators and presidents gain and lose their offices by how well the economy is doing under their leadership.

It is intriguing to see how leaders of the Religious Right began to concern themselves with the issue of a strong national defense in the late 1970s and early 1980s. Thirty years ago it became fashionable among political leaders and candidates to spout off about the need to cut government spending, namely, welfare spending. However, when conservative politicians were pushed to apply their fiscal conservatism to the area of national defense, they would often refuse to consider any cuts to those programs. In truth, conservative politicians are beholden to large defense contractors for hefty campaign contributions. These same politicians have no need to worry about the poor since they have no funds to contribute to the campaign chests of these budget surgeons.

I recall a meeting I had with then Congressman Phil Gramm of Texas, one of the original architects of the massive welfare cut plans in the early 1980s. During that meeting I challenged Congressman Gramm to cut waste in both social programs and defense spending. The congressman sidestepped the issue of cutting defense spending by making some vague allusion to the threat of communism and the need for a strong defense. Thus, the burden of balancing the budget would be placed completely upon social programs. National Defense budgets would be spared the harsh scalpel.

William Lloyd Allen says,

> The religious right today, in its overemphasis on issues like evolution and prayer in the schoolroom, arguments for accepting the nuclear arms race because peace will not come to earth until Jesus returns, unquestioning loyalty to the flag, and anticommunist fervor, is reminiscent of some 1934 Baptists. Indeed, some Baptists today claim these issues as the core of the Baptist heritage."[3]

In response to Allen's statement, I would go further to state that a vast majority of Baptists claim these issues as central concerns.

Throughout the last twenty years, the Religious Right has touted the term "traditional moral values" to speak of the moral issues they deem most important. In 1980 President Jimmy Carter professed to be a "born-again" Christian, taught Sunday School at the First Baptist Church of Washington, DC, and even witnessed to foreign diplomats about his faith, yet he was defeated by a former Hollywood actor, a divorcee, who said very little about his faith in any direct or convincing manner. The Religious Right greatly helped Ronald Reagan to gain the office of President of the United States. As I previously mentioned, waging peace and insuring economic justice for all were not issues that occupied any list of any of the voter guides provided by organizations representing the Religious Right.

As churches seek to grow numerically and financially, pastors do not sense the need to voice concern for the rights of the poorest in our society. Walter Rauschenbusch, however, expressed his pastoral sentiments in this way:

These [prophets] were almost indifferent, if not contemptuous, about the ceremonial side of customary religion, but turned with passionate enthusiasm to moral righteousness as the true domain of religion. Where would their interest lie if they lived today? Their religious concern was not restricted to private religion and morality, but dealt pre-eminently with the social and political life of their nation. Would they limit its range today? Their sympathy was wholly and passionately with the poor and oppressed. If they lived today, would they place the chief blame for poverty on the poor and give their admiration to the strong?[1]

When surfing the channels of religious programs today, it is impossible to locate a minister who is talking about social and economic justice. That issue is just not heard on television and radio broadcasting. That kind of preaching does not bring people in the doors by the droves, nor will that kind of preaching help raise the budget funds needed in order to build buildings, pay utilities, hire staff and fund a multitude of programs. The very contexts from which these television ministers preach exude opulence, wealth and abundance. One leading national religious network prominently features ornate gold furniture in its television production set. Everything about this set says "affluence and success."

In the late 1990s a popular national evangelist, Jesse Duplantis, released a newsletter that noted his intention to purchase a Citation X jet for use in world evangelism. The notice reads as follows:

Over five years ago, the Lord blessed us with a Citation Eagle jet, which made it possible for Jesse to preach to more people in USA than ever before. Jesse hung a sign in it that says, "God's been good to Jesse" and we thank God for it every day. So when the Lord began to deal with Jesse about believing Him for Citation X (10), a larger corporate jet with the speed and fuel capacity to fly anywhere in the world, he said, "But Lord, I don't want it. I'm satisfied."

God replied, "I'm not," and instructed Jesse to stretch his faith for his new jet. Why? Because it is a tool for World Evangelism and will enable Jesse to reach other nations of the world with the Gospel. As these last days draw to a close, it's time to speed up the work and answer the call to reach more nations for God.

As you read this vision, please take time to pray and believe God with us for this great tool for World Evangelism. Like Jesse says, "I didn't ask for it. God told me to believe for it!" So we are praying in obedience to God for JDM's CITATION X and know that He will bring it to pass! Glory![5]

The above solicitation is a prime example of truth becoming stranger than fiction. This is the stuff that parodies of evangelists are made of. In truth, it is just another of the many examples of the degree of dependence that American religious leaders have on a strong and growing economy and of their need for security. Issues surrounding social and economic justice are thus rendered non-existent in the consideration of a president. As long as the president provides more jobs, more income and more security, we can look the other way regarding justice and concern for human rights. This type of preoccupation with financial security has the potential of ushering in a society that is not only unjust, but also oppressive and abusive.

When citizens cannot obtain adequate food for their families, that is not only a societal problem, it is a national sin. When people of a nation cannot obtain housing for their families, it is not only a problem for those who are without shelter, it is an indictment on all who have a place to live. When citizens cannot obtain health care, it is a sin. Rauschenbusch is especially prophetic when he says in this regard,

If God stands for the present social order, how can we defend him? . . . We cannot stand for poor and laborious people being deprived of physical stature, youth education, human equality, and justice, in order to enable others to live luxurious lives. It revolts us to see these conditions perpetrated by law and organized force, and palliated or justified by the makers of public opinion. . . . A conception of God which describes him as sanctioning the present social order and utilizing it in order to sanctify its victims through their suffering, without striving for its overthrow, is repugnant to our moral sense.[6]

NOTES

1. Richard V. Pierard, "Radical Resistance," Christian History (Vol. X, No.4, 1991), 30.

2. William Lloyd Allen, "How Baptists assessed Hitler," Peacework (May-June/July-August 1987), 13.

3. Ibid., 13.

4. Walter Rauschenbusch, A Rauschenbusch Reader. Ed. by Benson Y. Landis (New York: Harper & Brothers, 1957), 9.

5. Jesse Duplantis, "Citation X: A Tool for World Evangelism," Voice of the Covenant (November 2000), 11.

6. Rauschenbusch, op. cit., 124–125.

CHAPTER 11

A RADICAL VIEW OF DISCIPLESHIP

There is a symbol which keeps me riveted to reality and that is quite simply the symbol of the Cross. You see, the Cross is laid on all people who dare to call themselves Christians. It is not the terrible end to an otherwise God-fearing and happy life. No. It meets us at the beginning of our communion with Christ. For when Christ calls a person, He bids that person to come and die.

THE SYMBOL OF THE CROSS is so much a part of our culture and so familiar to Christians that it is extremely difficult for us to view the cross in radical new ways. The German theologian Jürgen Moltmann has introduced the world to an entirely new and revolutionary perspective of the cross and thus opened the doors for new understanding of this ancient symbol. Moltmann seems to capture the theme to which Bonhoeffer was pointing; that is, that Christianity must completely reexamine the meaning of the cross in both doctrine and practice. In a quite remarkable passage he states:

> The church of the crucified was at first, and basically remains, the church of the oppressed and insulted, the poor and wretched, the church of the people. On the other hand, it is also the church of those who have turned away from their inward and external forms of domination and oppression . . . If it truly remembers the crucified Christ, it cannot allow a bland, religious indifference to prevail towards everyone. As the crucified Messiah, it is the church of liberation for all men (people), whether Jews or Gentiles, Greeks or barbarians, masters or ser-

vants, men or women . . . As the people of the crucified Christ, the church originated in the particular earthly events of the oppression and liberation of Jesus, and exists in the midst of a divided and mutually hostile world of inhuman people on one side and dehumanized people on the other.[1]

Dietrich Bonhoeffer's decision to place himself in danger of imprisonment and death was a decision to cast his lot with the victims rather than the victors. At the very base of all of Bonhoeffer's dangerous decisions was the figure of the crucified Jesus, the One who was victimized by the State. To participate in history for the downtrodden, the oppressed was to live out "costly grace." Bonhoeffer revealed this theological principle consistently through his correspondence from prison. In a statement he titled "Sympathy" he says,

> We are not Christ, but if we want to be Christians, we must have some share in Christ's large-heartedness by acting with responsibility and in freedom when the hour of danger comes, and by showing a real sympathy that springs, not from fear, but from the liberating and redeeming love of Christ for all who suffer. Mere waiting and looking on is not Christian behaviour. The Christian is called to sympathy and action, not in the first place by his own sufferings, but by the sufferings of his brethren, for whose sake Christ suffered.[2]

This statement seems to bring together the Christ who suffered and the responsible Christian's call to suffer for those who are oppressed. In other words, Bonhoeffer's motivations for action and decision-making were not political or ideological but Christological in foundation.

In a letter entitled "Thoughts on the Day of the Baptism of Dietrich Wilhelm Rudiger Bethge" dated May, 1944, Bonhoeffer states, "It will not be difficult for us to renounce our privileges recognizing the justice of history. We may have to face events and changes that take no account of our wishes and our rights. But if so, we shall not give way to embittered and barren pride, but consciously submit to divine judgment, and so prove ourselves worthy to survive by identifying ourselves generously and unselfishly with the life of the community and the sufferings of our fellow-men."[3]

A strong sense of Bonhoeffer's identification with the cross of Christ can be seen in a letter dated July 21, 1944, one day after the failed assassination attempt on Hitler. In this letter Bonhoeffer writes, "By this-worldliness I mean living unreservedly in life's duties, problems, successes and failures, experiences and perplexities. In so doing we throw ourselves completely into the arms of God, taking seriously, not our own sufferings, but those of God in the world-watching with Christ in Gethsemane. That, I think, is faith; that is metanoia . . ."[4]

Dietrich Bonhoeffer thrusts a radically different kind of cross image, first for the Christian, and secondly, for the entire world. This is not a cross of glory or triumphalism or power. This is a cross of suffering that identifies itself and the follower of Christ with the sufferings of the world. Bonhoeffer's view contrasts sharply with the "theological" view of Adolf Hitler who said, "I believe that I am acting in accordance with the will of the Almighty Creator: by defending myself against the Jew, I am fighting for the work of the Lord."[5] Hitler's view coincides closely with the misappropriation of the cross by the Ku Klux Klan as they burned crosses on the property of African-Americans and others who were sympathetic to African-Americans.

Bonhoeffer's remarkable new way of considering the meaning of the cross was a precursor to the challenges of Latin American Liberation Theologian, Jon Sobrino. In his profoundly moving and stimulating text *Christology at the Crossroads*, Sobrino writes:

Theological reflection on the cross of Jesus is very infrequent; and when it is carried out, it rarely reaches the level of showing that the cross and the proclamation of a "crucified God" embody the authentic originality of the Christian faith. Such reflection usually remains on the level of pious contemplation. It does not bring out the fact that the cross of Christ implies a new and revolutionary concept of God on both the theoretical and practical level.[6]

Sobrino goes on to discuss certain traditional and historical understandings of the cross and counters those views:

The danger of the explanatory models . . . is that they tend to interiorize salvation . . . the real problem is that they tend to treat salvation in terms of inner life, explaining how the cross can bring forgiveness for one's sins, while neglecting to treat of salvation in relationship to the world outside and the problems of externalized injustice and sinfulness.[7]

We do not find in Bonhoeffer's writings a thorough and detailed new "theology of the cross." What we do find is the beginning of a completely new perspective and, more importantly, the application of that new understanding by Bonhoeffer in the sacrifice of his life for this radical new concept. It would be left to a later generation and theologians such as Moltmann and Sobrino to further elucidate this new understanding of the cross event. What we learn from Bonhoeffer and these daring contemporary theologians is that to identify with Christ and the cross is to identify with those who suffer and to suffer with those who suffer. To identify with Christ and the cross means to release our embrace on the gods of success, power, triumph and exclusivism.

The Cross

The Cross
Simple
Crude
Ugly
Ghastly
Applied to common criminals; a punishment of humiliation,
of excruciating agony, of death; a tragic symbol of the crime
of all time, the crucifixion of the Son of God; epitome of
banishment, relegated to its place outside the gates.
The Cross,
atop stately
structures
of advanced
civilizations.
Now within
the city gates.
Worn by the
inhabitants
in gold, in
silver, with
diamonds.
Adorning
magnificent
edifices,
established
in society's
mainstream.
Massive
Shining
Artistic
Esthetic
Accepted
Co-opted

Peruvian theologian Gustavo Gutierrez, who has been called "the father of Latin American Liberation Theology," introduced the world to radically new interpretations of salvation which seem amazingly reminiscent of Bonhoeffer. He states, "Those who reduce the work of salvation are indeed those who limit it to the strictly 'religious' sphere and are not aware of the universality of the process. It is those who think that the work of Christ touches the social order in which we live only indirectly and tangentially, and not in its roots and basic structures. It is those who in order to protect salvation (or to protect their interests) lift salvation from the midst of history, where men and social classes struggle to liberate themselves from the slavery and oppression to which other men and social classes have subjected them."[8] The influence of Bonhoeffer's insights and his fulfillment of responsible action in history for the oppressed can be detected in Gutierrez's definition of conversion, as follows:

> A spirituality of liberation will center on a conversion to the neighbor, the oppressed person, the exploited social class, the despised race, the dominated country. Our conversion to the Lord implies conversion to the neighbor. Evangelical conversion is indeed the touchstone of all spirituality. Conversion means a radical transformation of ourselves; it means thinking, feeling, and living as Christ-present in exploited and alienated man. To be converted is to commit oneself to the process of the liberation of the poor and oppressed, to commit oneself lucidly, realistically, and concretely. It means to commit oneself not only generously, but also with an analysis of the situation and a strategy of action...our conversion process is affected by the socioeconomic, political, cultural, and human environment in which it occurs. Without a change in these structures, there is no authentic conversion. We have to break with our mental categories, with the way we relate to others, with our way of identifying with the Lord, with our cultural milieu, with our

social class, in other words, with all that can stand in the way of a real, profound solidarity with those who suffer, in the first place, from misery and injustice. Only thus, and not through purely interior and spiritual attitudes, will the "new man" arise from the ashes of the "old."[9]

Dietrich Bonhoeffer's statements on the cross and his martyrdom, which gave validity to those statements, provided the theological precedent in both principle and practice, doctrine and deed, theory and application, to the bold challenges that would later come from liberation theologians. Bonhoeffer's words and deeds not only served to influence "The Theology of Liberation." They also serve as a challenge to Western Christianity where success, influence, wealth and power still play a major and dominant role in our understanding of the nature of the cross.

NOTES

1. Jürgen Moltmann, *The Crucified God* (New York: Harper & Row, 1974), 52–53.

2. Dietrich Bonhoeffer, *Letters and Papers from Prison* (New York: Macmillan, 1971), 14.

3. Ibid., 299.

4. Ibid., 370.

5. Christopher M. Leighton, Prologue to *Mature Christianity in the 21st Century* by Norman A. Beck (New York: Crossroad, 1994), 22.

6. Jon Sobrino, *Christology at the Crossroads* (Maryknoll: Orbis, 1982), 179.

7. Ibid., 190.

8. Gustavo Gutierrez, *A Theology of Liberation* (Maryknoll: Orbis, 1981), 177–178.

9. Ibid., 204–5.

BIBLIOGRAPHY

Allen, William Lloyd. How Baptists Assessed Hitler. *Peacework*. May-June/July–August 1973.

Beck, Norman A. *Mature Christianity in the 21st Century*. New York: Crossroad, 1994.

Bethge, Eberhard. *Dietrich Bonhoeffer*. New York: Harper & Row, 1985.

Blumenthal, David R. *Facing the Abusing God: A Theology of Protest*. Louisville: Westminster/John Knox Press, 1993.

Bonhoeffer, Dietrich. *Ethics*. New York: Macmillan, 1986.

———. *Letters and Papers from Prison*. New York: Macmillan, 1971.

Brown, Robert McAfee. *Elie Wiesel: Messenger to All Humanity*. Notre Dame: University of Notre Dame Press, 1989.

Duplantis, Jesse. Citation X: A Tool for World Evangelism. *Voice of the Covenant*. November 2000.

Gutierrez, Gustavo. *A Theology of Liberation*. Maryknoll: Orbis, 1981.

Kelly, Geffrey. Bonhoeffer and Romero. *Theology and the Practice of Responsibility*. Edited by Wayne Whitson Floyd Jr. and Charles Marsh. Valley Forge: Trinity Press International, 1994.

Lee, Dallas. *The Cotton Patch Evidence*. Americus: Koinonia Partners, 1971.

Leighon, Christopher M. Prologue. In Beck, Norman A. *Mature Christianity in the 21st Century*. New York: Crossroad, 1994.

Lowell, James Russell. *The Vision of Sir Launfal and Other Poems*. Boston: Houghton Mifflin, 1905.

Marable, Manning. The Politics of Inequality. *The Black World Today*. January 2001.

Merton, Thomas. *Witness to Freedom*. Edited by William H. Shannon. New York: Harcourt Brace & Company, 1994.

Metz, Johann Baptist. *The Emergent Church*. New York: Crossroad, 1981.

Moltmann, Jürgen. *The Crucified God*. New York: Harper & Row, 1974.

Nicholls, William. *Christian Antisemitism: A History of Hate.* Northvale: Jason Aronson, 1995.

Perry, Marvin and Frederick M. Schweitzer, eds. *Jewish-Christian Encounters over the Centuries.* New York: Peter Lang, 1994.

Pierard, Richard V. Radical Resistance. *Christian History.* X, 4. (1991).

Rauschenbusch, Walter. *A Rauschenbusch Reader.* Edited by Benson Y. Landis. New York: Harper & Brothers, 1957.

Rohr, Richard. *Radical Grace.* Cincinnati: St. Anthony Messenger Press, 1993.

Romero, Oscar. *The Violence of Love.* Translated and Edited by James R. Brockman. Farmington: The Plough Publishing Company, 1988.

Sobrino, Jon. *Christology at the Crossroads.* Maryknoll: Orbis, 1982.

Wiesel, Elie. *Memoirs: All Rivers Run to the Sea.* New York: Schocken, 1995.

———. *The Trial of God.* New York: Schocken, 1979.